PRAISE

Raffi brings to the debate on the benefits and dangers of the digital revolution his well-known sense of compassion, concern and hope. *Lightweb Darkweb* is the ultimate example of self-regulation: a desperately needed message that we need to think seriously about how we use the extraordinary power that has been unleashed in order to educate and inspire, without exposing our children to the perils that are also so pervasive. This is a book that every one of us needs to read.

Stuart Shanker, Distinguished Research Professor of Philosophy and Psychology, York University

Raffi Cavoukian's twin passions for children and the planet shine through in *Lightweb Darkweb*, a smart, highly readable and nuanced critique of society's unquestioning embrace of social media. This is an important book for anyone who cares about the well-being of the youngest and most vulnerable among us.

Susan Linn, director of the Campaign for a Commercial-Free Childhood, instructor in psychiatry, Harvard Medical School

Generations of children and parents have grown up listening to Raffi. Now they can listen once again as he describes how to make the digital world safe, secure and nurturant—emotionally and intellectually. *Lightweb Darkweb* presents a deeply felt argument that insists we act in the best interests of the next generation. Raffi thinks we owe our children no less, and he is right.

Sherry Turkle, psychologist, MIT professor, author of *Alone Together: Why We Expect More from Technology and Less from Each Other*

At once passionate and level-headed, Raffi's timely book provides parents and kids with a much-needed guide to the highways, byways and back streets of the social web.

Nicholas Carr, author of *The Shallows* and *The Big Switch*

To the many enthusiasts who have heralded social media as a revolutionary outburst of freedom, community and knowledge, Raffi offers a clear retort: "The medium is the problem." *Lightweb Darkweb* is written by a man with a lifelong devotion to healthy childhood. Adults who have grown up listening to Raffi will profit from his reflections on the uncertain consequences of the digital age. All that makes us love digital tools has a dark side, Raffi warns, which, unless recognized, risks our children's physical, intellectual and emotional well-being.

Mark Bauerlein, Emory University professor, author of *The Dumbest Generation* and editor of *The Digital Divide*

Raffi reminds all of us of the importance of thinking critically about digital technologies before we blindly consume them. *Lightweb Darkweb* speaks to the very pressing need for widespread digital and consumer literacy. This is something we all can benefit from.

Jaigris Hodson, researcher and instructor, Ryerson University

Raffi is an extraordinary advocate and creator for children. This book has a great message for all of us, young and old. Read it.

James P. Steyer, founder and CEO of Common Sense Media, author of *Talking Back to Facebook*

Whether you're a parent, teacher or young person, this book is required reading to skillfully navigate the wonderful and dangerous world of social media. *Lightweb Darkweb* explains the challenges and offers ways forward. Please turn off your screen and pick up this book!

Annie Leonard, author of *The Story of Stuff*

Raffi artfully implores us to be decision makers and bring our humanity to this new digital realm.

Douglas Rushkoff, media theorist, author of
Present Shock: When Everything Happens Now

Bravo! Raffi alerts us to the risks of unintended consequences in the online world, including the loss of control, without which there can be no privacy. *Lightweb Darkweb* provides a great service in raising this vital issue for all to consider.

Dr Ann Cavoukian, Privacy Commissioner of Ontario

Raffi Cavoukian is both a popular troubadour and a keen social analyst with well-founded concerns about how the social media are affecting children. *Lightweb Darkweb* raises the questions that communications policy makers should long since have raised—and answered.

Lester Brown, president, Earth Policy Institute,
author of *Full Planet, Empty Plates*

The message in *Lightweb Darkweb* is compelling. Raffi issues a call to action that's hard to ignore—he begins a conversation that everyone interested in kids using social media needs to be part of.

Gwenn Schurgin O'Keeffe, MD, FAAP, author of *CyberSafe*

In this passionate book, Raffi raises profound questions about our responsibilities—as parents, educators, citizens—for the healthy development of young children and for the long-term survival of our planet.

Howard Gardner, Harvard professor, author (with Katie Davis) of *The App Generation: How Young People Navigate Identity, Intimacy, and Imagination in the Digital Age*

What a joy it is to read the heartfelt and profound insights about social media from the man who entertained and delighted our children! Raffi's commitment to kids is palpable in these pages. I hope all those who care about children take his central messages to heart.

Dr Dimitri Christakis, director, Center for Child Health, Behavior and Development at Seattle Children's Hospital

#lightwebdarkweb

Also by Raffi Cavoukian

The Life of a Children's Troubadour (1999)
Homeland Press

Child Honouring:
How to Turn This World Around (2006)
co-edited with Sharna Olfman
Homeland Press

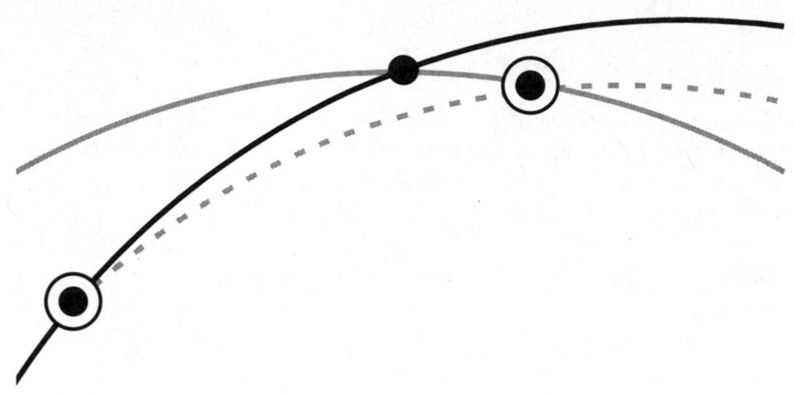

Lightweb Darkweb

Three Reasons To Reform Social Media
Be4 It Re-Forms Us

Raffi Cavoukian

Homeland
Press

Library and Archives Canada Cataloguing in Publication
Raffi, author
Lightweb Darkweb / Raffi Cavoukian.

Includes bibliographical references and index.
Issued in print and electronic formats.
ISBN 978-0-9866446-1-0 (pbk.).--ISBN 978-0-9866446-2-7 (ebook)

1. Internet and children. 2. Social media--Moral and ethical aspects. 3. Social media--Security measures. 4. Online social networks--Moral and ethical aspects. 5. Online social networks--Security measures. I. Title.
HQ784.I58R34 2013 025.042'083 C2013-903395-5
C2013-903396-3

Published in Canada by Homeland Press,
a division of Troubadour Music.
www.raffinews.com

Printed and bound in Canada by Friesens
Design and layout by Ande Axelrod Graphic Design

The chlorine bleaching of pulp for paper produces toxic compounds that go into our air and water and end up in human blood and breast milk. One way to reduce the output of dioxin, among the most lethal of these poisons, is to bleach paper with a process using hydrogen peroxide. Since toxic compounds most threaten the very young, we have a duty to use toxic-free manufacturing processes. As we all continue to turn to benign alternatives, the costs of polluting technologies will no longer be hidden. Before long, sustainable means will become the moral standard for all our endeavours.

This book was printed on Rolland Enviro 100 FSC paper, containing 100% post-consumer fibre and processed chlorine-free. The text was printed with vegetable-based inks. All adhesives are solvent-free.

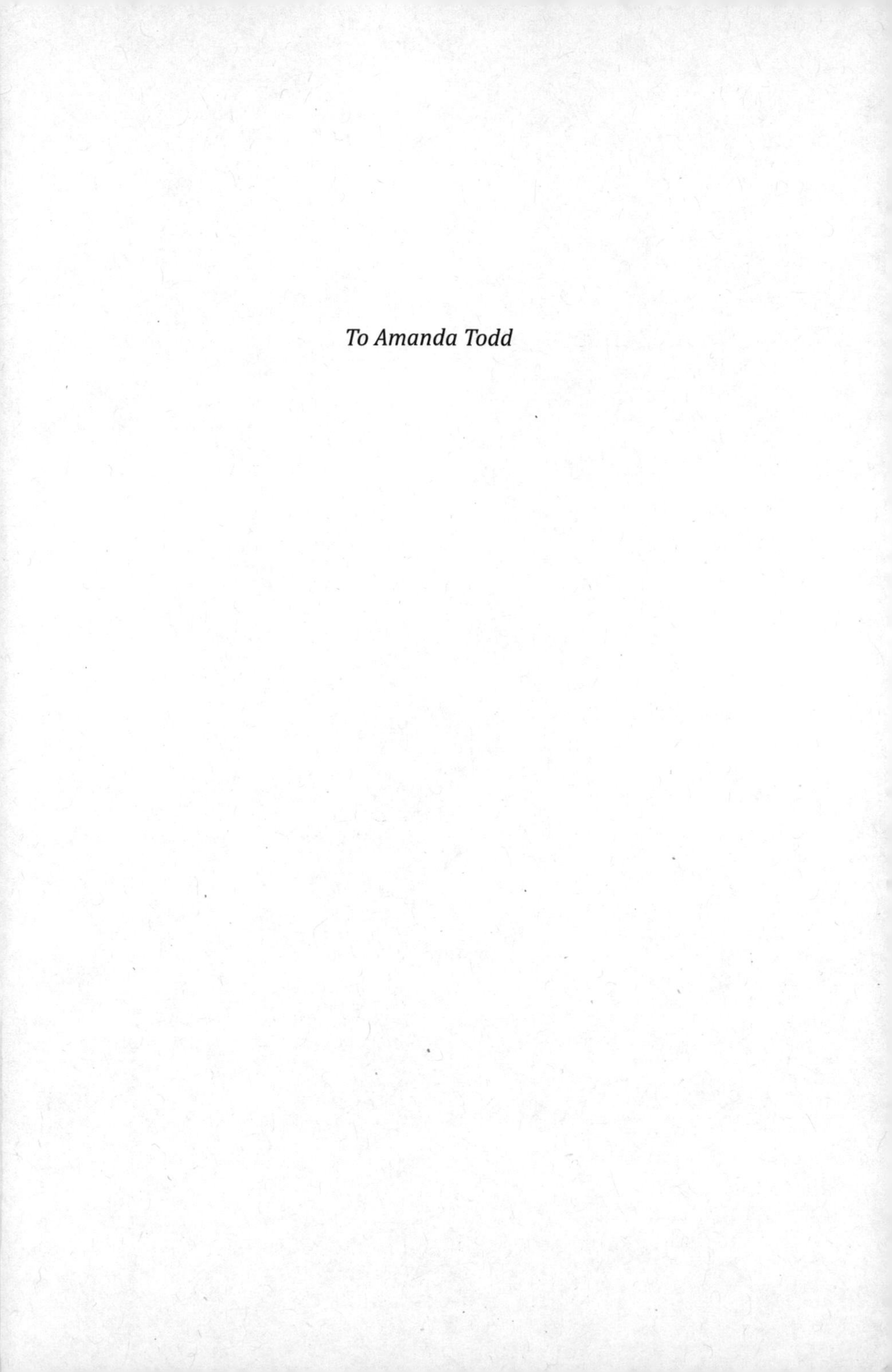

To Amanda Todd

CONTENTS

This world is but a canvas to our imagination.
Henry David Thoreau

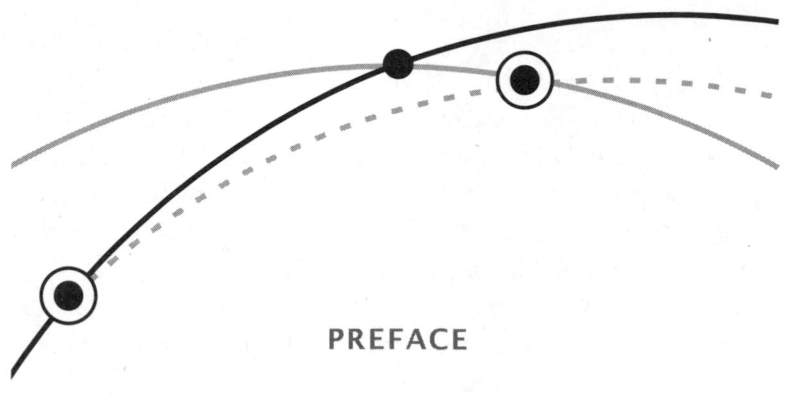

PREFACE

AS A TROUBADOUR and tech enthusiast, as an ecology advocate and children's champion, I'm moved to comment on what I sense is an opportunity and crisis of epochal proportions: a chance to optimize the social and environmental benefits of a digitally connected global village by acting quickly to subdue the perils of InfoTech's shadow.

The worldwide web of computer connection has a light side and a dark side.

The "Lightweb" is known to all who use the Internet as a daily part of life. We easily connect to anyone around the world, not just via email, but through a variety of online platforms and texting applications even on the smallest personal computing devices; we have access to a global storehouse of information; powerful search engines find documents, arguments and historical precedents, and almost any online question finds answers; we connect by audio and video with anyone, for free; we can build an online music and entertainment library without leaving home; we have palm-sized devices with dazzling capabilities for learning, recording, sharing and connecting.

The "Darkweb" is there too. Imposters, predators and porn sites lurk in the shadows on the Information Superhighway and all too easily lure unsuspecting users; identity theft is an issue, as is the loss of privacy due to the "data mining" practices of social media companies; online platforms allow stalkers to find the addresses and phone numbers of unwary users who are bullied, shamed and harassed mercilessly; the hundreds of millions of young users who were never intended to be on social media (SM) are the most vulnerable to security breaches, sometimes with lethal consequences.

Net evangelists cheer the virtual world with little reservation. Yet while there's scant evidence that daily online engagement contributes to, say, character development in our young, we do have evidence of Net dependence and SM addiction, with negative impacts on personal wellbeing and productivity.

The SM crisis is hard to miss: If kids (the unintended users for whom the Net was not designed) aren't safe on social media, if they can't effectively avoid the worst of the Darkweb, we've got a social catastrophe—a growing challenge to physical and mental health. The opportunity, simply put, is this: If social media is reformed with systemic safety features, if parents and teachers put sensible limits on screen time and age restrictions on Net use, we just might make the best of a very tough situation: *benefit from the Lightweb by minimizing its shadow.*

Is this possible? Can we regulate and inspire a digital code of conduct that rewards our highest inclinations and enables connecting for the greatest good?

If you make it past the next four paragraphs, we might well have a conversation. I'd like that very much.

Imagine a highway with no speed limits and no guard rails, where vehicles have no seatbelts and faulty brakes, and drivers (many of them underage) are constantly distracted—that's the Information Superhighway. Would you rush to give your kids a sports car to drive on that highway—a smartphone? Hardly. You would at least wait until they were old enough to have a driver's licence.

PREFACE

Imagine parenting challenges with a quarter to a third of families led by a single parent; where even two-parent families have a hard time making ends meet; where kids now socialize virtually, texting their peers constantly—welcome to parenting in the 21st century. Harder than ever.

Imagine a pop culture that exploits the young by targeting them for logo identification from birth, relentlessly marketing and advertising to them; a culture that sexualizes young girls, that glorifies violence and uses sex to sell anything—that's the hyper-sexualized (what some call "pornified") pop culture in which our kids grow up.

Imagine a planet with a global economy on shaky ground, life support systems in peril, species going extinct at record rates and runaway climate change threatening life as we know it. That's the world we're living in—a polluted one in which babies worldwide are born with a body burden of toxic chemicals.

The global village—McLuhan's prescient term—is in a state of emergency: on the brink of breakdown or, perhaps, breakthrough. If I could wave a Harry Potter wand, I'd summon a grand new ethic to wake us from the Muggle doldrums to our higher sensibilities. I'd conjure a new economic model that might reverse the "money-above-all-else" bottom-line fixation that's killing planetary life supports and poisoning our world. I'd wish for a startling new discovery that could restore the tainted present and reverse the rush into depleted and frightening futures.

Some think digital technology is that magic wand. I believe that in its present form it adds to our problems as much as helps us.

This book provides three good reasons to reform social media and, along the way, rethink our relationship with the Information Superhighway and its "shiny tech" devices. The reasons are Safety, Intelligence, Sustainability.

Part 1 of this book, "Safety," looks at the vulnerability of SM users, especially the young. Part 2, "Intelligence," deals with the pros and cons of "digitally enhanced" living. Part 3, "Sustainability," sheds light on the ecology of InfoTech, something we don't hear much about. The global context? A world with much economic instability and an ominous climate threat.

What the daunting big picture says to me is that we need something other than tech miracles in a ramped-up digital culture. I'm as happy to see tech innovation as the next person, so long as such innovation is socially sound and environmentally benign. As many have said, what humanity needs is a new ecological consciousness—to transcend the myopic shortcomings of our mechanistic past. To me, what the world needs most is to embrace the global ethic we call sustainability, well-known in some circles but hardly a household word in our corporate-dominated societies.

Reforming social media without delay is critical. Without SM reform we doom ourselves to distraction, tweeting on the new *Titanic*. The right reforms now can give us the best chance of harnessing our Net inclinations to create a culture of true connection: a culture of respect for Earth and all her children. Without that, I fear for our future.

The conversation we need to have is time sensitive. Let's talk.

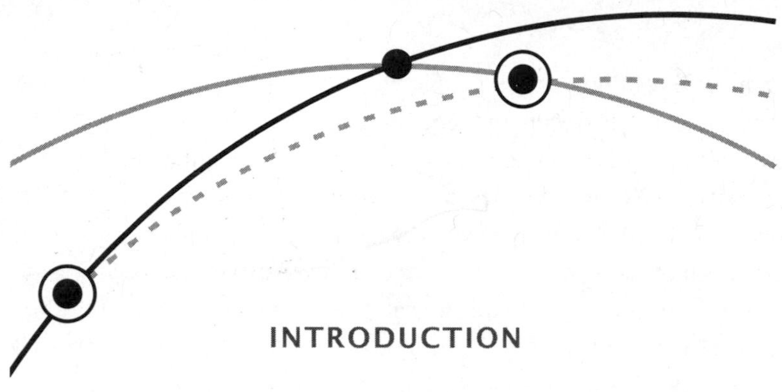

INTRODUCTION

I AM A social media user questioning the widespread obsession with SM. After only nine short years this emerging technology-turned-habit has dramatically affected childhood, family relations and adolescent experience. My concern is primarily with SM's effect on young users, but it has also had an impact on adults. The Info Superhighway has made us drunk with knowledge and changed the pulse of our lives. We need a sobriety test or, at the very least, a reality check.

We are undergoing a vast social experiment—one in which, for the first time, our young are growing up in two worlds: real and virtual. Previously, we'd speak of "real and imaginary," but the imaginary worlds kids created in the past were nothing like the virtual world they are finding, ready-made, online. They were of children's own imaginings.

Social media virtuality and tech devices represent the greatest intrusion on child development since TV—a far greater intrusion, because they are more fun, and pervasive. Babies today will grow up in families that have a number of shiny tech screens. While we have no data indicating this is a good thing, we have many reasons for concern.

Humans have always lived in relation to Nature, although the industrial revolution's gains came with considerable costs: our planet ravaged, species decimated, people alienated from Nature. Now the proliferation of personal electronic devices may amplify an already worrisome "Nature deficit" for the young, who grow up in thrall to screen culture. The authority of the multi-dimensional organic world has been transferred to its shiny tech representations, which engage more than our screen experience. They alter our sense of reality. They affect our brains. For parents struggling to balance their real family life with the virtual, it's a big challenge. And all of this leaves child development experts in a quandary, unsure how to respond to such rapid social change.

iConnect

IN 2010 I made my Twitter debut. After my initial scoffing at 140-character communication, I thought I'd try it. Turned out to be great fun! I met interesting people, got world news at electric speed and shared my thoughts and feelings with a growing audience of "tweeps." To this songwriter, the limited message length was no problem. You can convey a lot in a short tweet and include links, photos or videos. Twitter's been fun, but I must admit: I've played less music, read fewer books and done less meditating. Social media takes a lot of one's time.

I manage my online time the best I can. As with my unlisted phone number, I don't give out my email address because I don't want hundreds of emails to sort through each morning, as some of my colleagues say they must do. (Can't imagine that daybreak drudgery.) My Skype name is also private, and this helps keep the number of such contacts manageable.

Also in 2010, after proudly making do for years with an older, semi-functioning flip mobile, I quickly embraced a multi-function smartphone that might as well be called iWorld for the breadth of what it offers. In my hand is access to a world of information, music, imagery and connectivity. For a connection lover like me, it's simply amazing.

I believe we all crave connection—with Creation, with life essence and with a circle of belonging. That craving now drives us to connect online, where connection junkies find comfort. We want to belong. We long for that feeling.

For young SM users, it's no different. Tweens and teens are developing a social self-image, taking subtle and overt societal cues about how to present themselves as desirable young men and women. Real connections with the people in their lives can be negatively impacted by the Darkweb of SM distortions. What is critically important is that, online, young SM users need to protect their privacy and engage safely, with discernment.

How I Use Digital Tech

AS IT HAS done for hundreds of millions of users, digital technology has certainly changed my own work and life habits. I want to share this to let you know the tech enthusiast position from which I critique the current digital mania.

When I'm songwriting, I often use the Sound Studio program on my MacBook Pro laptop for "demo-ing" a new song idea. (For just guitar and voice, I like this app; it's much simpler than Garage Band.) One-touch recording captures the basic song idea right away. And I can edit easily as needed within the visually displayed recorded passage. Playback is easy. Forward and backward location is easy. It's all so easy: no audiotape, just sounds. I do as many test songs or song idea performances as I want, as there's lots of memory for saving these. And I'm so glad I can just email these "demos" and get prompt feedback. Gone is the hassle of sending audio-cassettes by courier.

I now mostly record without that large physical recording console of days gone by—it's done on my audio engineer's laptop recording software with its multi-track record and mix visuals. (As producer Daniel Lanois has shown, mobile recording brings "the studio" to any place you want.) We often record in my living room, with mikes hooked into a small pre-amp box connected to a laptop. Mixing is easy with precise pre-recorded elements that the program flawlessly memorizes, saves and replays. (Automated mixing, as we used to say in analog days.) The numerical calibrations are displayed on the laptop screen, flowing left to right in measured time intervals. Razor-sharp edits are done (and undone) without razors, with just the clicks of a mouse.

For all my fond nostalgia for the good old analog days of 24-track tape machines (sometimes two of these connected and synced to operate as one), I don't miss those costly hassle-filled days. Nor do I miss the kinks of vinyl album pressings that were prone to warping, tics and pops, sound distortion, and scratches enough to drive me, an indie label president, bonkers. I still recall my astonished jaw-dropped reaction when the A&M Records brass in Toronto first played me a CD in the mid-80s. No static, no noise—just pure sound. Loved it.

Nowadays, in my essay and book writing, the laptop is king. Good thing I took typing in grade nine! Nothing better than typing fast when you're putting ideas on the screen page. That said, I so love the feel of my fountain pen on paper when I want to get away from it all (my laptop, I mean) and do some penmanship.

Researching online at electric speed is magic. I'm astonished with the breadth of what's available via search engines such as Google on almost any topic. Books and articles quickly appear, and commentary, analysis, reviews and YouTube talks are all at my fingertips. Idea shopping via "TED talks" or just by searching for someone's name in YouTube offers a wide range of opinion. Same for searching by a theme, question or concern—you get a huge selection of pertinent information. From quinoa salad recipes to the history of a Beatles recording to a current film review, it's all there and much more. You could spend most of your time online, it's that tantalizing. Too much of this at any given time does zone you out, as many know.

You can watch news happening and history being made online. And SM has played a crucial role in some events. In fact, my going on Twitter was partly inspired by Egypt's "Arab Spring" in January 2010. I was moved by the heroic freedom wave in Cairo, my birthplace. To mark SM's role in that triumph I recorded the tongue-in-cheek tribute "Tweet Me Right (The Cairo Tango)"—"Here or Tahrir, tweet me right, near or far tweet me right." People need respect. They'll risk dying for that dignity.

Skype has become another online feature I enjoy. Skype audio calls not only replace talking with a telephone handset; they also let you search online any topic that comes up in real time, during the conversation. Video Skype visits are great fun and can be very useful. A friend travelling or stationed on the other side of the world is magically right there on your screen. You can gain an impression of a potential employee that's otherwise not available—not to take the place of a resumé, references or a piece of writing, but to enhance your sense of the person.

As families know, Skype video is great for connecting with relatives both near and far. For single-parent families whose kids shuttle back and forth between mom and dad, a Skype video visit can be a touchstone with the parent who is not there. And little kids can have a glimpse of out-of-town grandparents on a regular basis. The Skype service thus far is free to users like me, touch wood. I'm really glad it's there.

By Skype (and other similar services), videoconferencing, once the stuff of science fiction, is now routine. Screen sharing is another online marvel that allows easy info sharing and collaboration. And Skype enables carbon-free live appearances too. In my home community, the Salt Spring Forum once featured a guest speaker from England, the journalist George Monbiot, who made his appearance by Skype. His talk went very well, as did the moderated Q & A the packed audience enjoyed.

Bananaphone to Smartphone

BACK IN THE mid-90s I used an early Mac computer for writing, but I wasn't online. My 1994 satirical song "Bananaphone" rang out "Don't need computers or TV to have a real good time!" For my fans, that "phone with a peel" became a beloved imaginary toy. Asked if I'd do a video of the song, I said no, not needed. In 1995 I recorded a CD called *Raffi Radio*. It was a pretend radio show to stimulate a child's theatre of imagination. The show was from a mythical place called Troubadoria. At a time of video's emerging dominance of home entertainment, I championed audio and its power to fire the imagination.

How quickly things have changed! Before I could respond to the ubiquitous minivan backseat DVD players and kids' escalating screen time, miniature computers brought the world into the palm of our hand.

It didn't take long for my "Banana" brand to face fierce competition from Apple. The iPhone I bought two years ago is always nearby because, like a Swiss Army knife, it has many functions. And that, my friends, is an understatement. It comes with a flashlight, handy when I go out at night on the dark country roads of the island where I live. And no need to wear a watch: This "phone" keeps time, wakes me up in the morning or from a nap, reminds me it's time for my next meeting and lets me meditate for a set period. It even has a stopwatch—as well as a compass, weather forecasts, GPS, Skype and great apps like a guitar tuner and a moon tracker. The GPS is a great help in reaching unfamiliar destinations, as my current car doesn't have GPS. When out for a walk I love to tune in to my iTunes collection of music (on headphones) or to my fave CBC radio programming. The iPhone offers news headlines on my browser or on Twitter, complete with video clips. That's why that pesky smartphone is so handy. Oh, and texting, did I mention that?

• • •

What is the compelling urgency of the machine that it can so intrude itself into the very stuff out of which man builds his world?
~ Joseph Weizenbaum, *Computer Power and Human Reason*

In 1995, I was invited by physicist and author Fritjof Capra of the Center for Ecoliteracy to take part in a conference, *Computers in Education: A Critical Look*. It was a robust two days of balancing the benefits of computer technology with kids' needs for learning in the real world. Among the recommendations I clearly recall: no computers before age 7, and minimal computer use from 7 to 14.

Among the presenters was Joseph Weizenbaum, the computer scientist who created ELIZA, a natural language program that could communicate with its user, and author of the 1976 book *Computer Power and Human Reason*.[1] "No other organism, and certainly no computer, can be made to confront genuine human problems in human terms," he wrote in that book. This pioneer of computer technology had misgivings about artificial intelligence. At MIT, one of his colleagues was psychologist and sociologist Sherry Turkle, who today continues to sound a caution about expecting less from people and more from technology. In her book *The Second Self*, Turkle writes: "Weizenbaum fears that the psychological theories that might be derived from artificial intelligence would lead to a flattened, mechanical view of human nature." She also noted Weizenbaum's idea that "what is essentially human is the uncodable."[2]

Uncodable. That's what children are. The essence of being human is most visible in the young of our species: that playful, spontaneous intelligence of pure heart and great wit.

Who could have imagined that I'd go from writing a 1994 children's song about a digital device of the information low-way to writing this cautionary book on its nemesis! Or that the little children who were (and are) my fans would grow up so quickly to be captivated by the wild web of the Internet with all its offerings and seductions, its promise and peril.

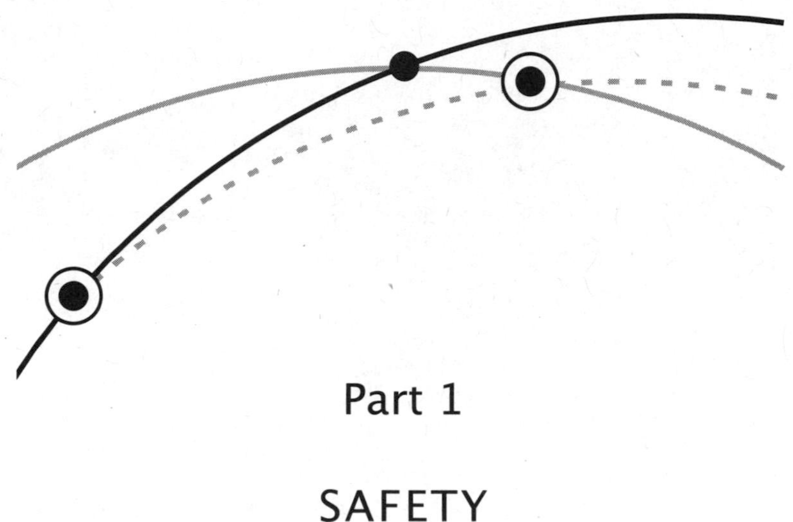

Part 1

SAFETY

Open Letter to Facebook

A TEEN SUICIDE near Vancouver, BC, alerted people worldwide to the cyberbullying that many young users of SM experience. Before ending her life after being stalked by a sexual predator and enduring years of public humiliation online, Amanda Todd posted a video on YouTube, and millions have viewed this farewell message of pain. Her death at 15 saddened and angered me. Vancouver community advocate Sandy Garossino and I co-wrote an open letter to Facebook COO Sheryl Sandberg, exhorting her to lead the SM industry with systemic changes for young user safety. Carol Todd, Amanda's mother, was among the signatories of the open letter, which said, in part:

> Known security gaps in a proliferating host of mobile applications have converted mainstream social media sites into highly effective devices for predators and abusive bullies. And in what can only be described as the cruelest irony, YouTube now sells advertising on Amanda's desperate video cry for help, while in a well-documented trend, her Facebook memorial page was desecrated.
>
> Facebook has become a brand feared by parents, when it should be one they can trust. We appeal to you as COO of Facebook, a mother, a visionary digital media leader, and member of the board of The Walt Disney Company, to lead industry-wide adoption of systemic security to block predators and abusers from accessing kids on major social media platforms, starting with Facebook itself.[1]

This open letter did not receive a reply, and SM safety concerns have only become more worrisome. Some of the better-known safety issues for SM users include loss of privacy, cyberbullying and shaming, location identification, data mining (companies gathering data on users so they can target ads or product offers they think will be of interest), social engineering (gaining people's trust to extract personal or private information, such as passwords), identity theft, creeping (online stalking, where someone gathers information on a person by studying their SM profiles and updates) and underage sexting (sharing sexually explicit images). More broadly worrying is the rapidly emerging issue of WiFi microwave radiation as a public health threat, especially for children, and the expanding intrusion of state and corporate surveillance on individual liberty, both of which I explore later in Part 1.

Red Hood Project

NOT LONG AFTER Amanda Todd's death, Sandy Garossino asked if I wanted to join her in starting a grassroots movement for cyber safety for young users. Along with Mark Busse (of communications design company Industrial Brand) and the Centre for Child Honouring (which I founded in 2010 on Salt Spring Island, BC), we co-founded Red Hood Project—a movement urging the SM industry to institute systemic safety for young users.

Garossino, a former lawyer and Crown prosecutor, insists that billion-dollar SM companies that create the risks for young users need to show corporate social responsibility. *They* must bear the burden for user safety, not the young. I agree.

Sandy and I co-wrote an op-ed that ran on various online sites. We expressed our dismay at both the lack of transparency in SM and the dangers that young users still face:

We are social media enthusiasts who care deeply about protecting vulnerable young users in the cyber woods from the predators out to get them.

The benefits of social media in connecting users worldwide are well known, and we ourselves have cheered the democratization of knowledge and information sharing. However, the proliferations of SM access to an increasingly younger demographic is most worrisome.

Our concern is with young SM users, the estimated 200 million under-17 users of Facebook and similar sites. Amanda Todd's call for help burns our senses and we shout a cry. And a challenge.

We cry foul, that SM providers still enable predators to easily find young victims online. We challenge social media businesses, multi-billion-dollar operations, to show some heart. We challenge Facebook, YouTube, Twitter and all such SM companies to soul searching. And real action.

From the start, these free services lacked transparency. We found out after the fact that we were being "data mined," our personal information and online history made available to advertisers to strategically target us with customized ads. We submitted to lengthy "Terms of Use" agreements that most people don't read.

Let's face it, we've been had, seduced by the world at our fingertips. Now we know better, that the dance was not free, the costs have been considerable.

As shocking as Amanda's story was, there is still much cause for worry. Known security gaps in a proliferating host of mobile applications have converted mainstream SM sites into highly effective devices for predators and abusive bullies...

Clearly, there is a security gap for young online users, a gap that is best addressed by those businesses that profit from offering SM services. They created the risk for young users. It is their corporate responsibility to build young user safety into all applications as a mandatory design requirement.[2]

With a Facebook (FB) page and @RedHoodProject Twitter handle, Sandy and I launched Red Hood on November 14, 2012, live on CKNW, a Vancouver radio station. Show host Bill Good, on hearing our pitch, joined us, as have hundreds of supportive people and organizations.

On the CBC Radio program *Q*, Sandy debated Internet safety with Internet privacy lawyer Parry Aftab, a safety advisor to Facebook. When Parry expressed the view that FB is doing all it can and that parents need to take responsibility for their kids' online safety, Sandy pointed out that, in the case of Amanda Todd,

> what was fairly obvious was that there had been such a serious breach of… security in the sense that an adult sexual predator was able to target, stalk, reach out and contact Amanda through her Facebook page... That someone was able to do that, leap over any of the security, which is almost nonexistent, was a real concern to me…
>
> We believe that this is a consumer protection issue. We believe that what children are using online should be protected under the Canada Consumer Protection Act. It largely governs physical objects that expose people and users and children to risk, and we want to see the protections of that Act extend to software. To me it's a perfect example of the gaps in social media. Although Parry claims that Facebook has the minimum age of 13, millions and millions of children younger than 13 are using Facebook and are using Instagram because Facebook and Instagram have no way of checking for ages.
>
> My concern is that we should be looking much more closely at the consumer protections, the product liability involved in, not only Facebook, but all social media, and that this should be a secure environment for kids. Because parents aren't really capable of navigating

> this landscape; it's become far to chaotic, far too difficult for them. As much as we applaud education and believe in education and believe in the "reporting model," it's clearly not up to the task at hand.[3]

As you read this book, I'd ask you to keep in mind that the needed level of parental oversight of kids' online habits is simply not practical, or possible, for most parents (see the section "A Mother's Concern" below). While parents can and must set limits for their kids' time online, set privacy settings on devices and teach their children respectful and safe online behaviour, parental supervision alone can't ensure safety for young SM users.

Unintended Audience

IN 2004, THE online platform started by Mark Zuckerberg and friends became Facebook, now the SM choice of an estimated 1 billion users. The irony is that FB doesn't put you face to face with anyone. It's an online way to share your life with family and friends, your virtual "friends" community and/or the world. What has caught us off guard is the millions of young users of SM under the age of 17.

Increasingly, people are questioning whether the online obsession, from Internet browsing to constant texting, is good for kids. SM is changing family life, youth peer relations and how people experience life. Yet we don't know the impact of such a quick and dramatic change in social norms. *We have no clear evidence that this is a good thing.*

We do have evidence it's a bad thing. In the wake of a public outcry over online bullying and many predator-driven teen suicides, we're scrambling to safeguard kids' time online. It should never have come to this.

Furthermore, in 2011, Mark Zuckerberg said that he wanted to make FB available to kids younger than 13, the company's current requirement for minimum user age. Incredibly, he seems to equate this with promoting education, saying, "My philosophy is that for education you need to start at a really, really young age."[4]

Equally hard to believe is the proposal by Maryland Attorney General Douglas Gansler to protect current Facebook users under 13 *within* that platform: "We would like to see Facebook create a safe space for kids to [use the site], a sanctuary, with the extra protections needed to ensure a safe, healthy, and age appropriate environment."[5] Quite the odd notion when Facebook instead should focus on explaining to parents and kids that the site isn't appropriate for use by children under 13.

"'We don't have the proper science and social research to evaluate the potential pros and cons that social-media platforms are doing to teenagers,' said James Steyer, founder and CEO of Common Sense Media, a child-advocacy group based in San Francisco. 'The idea that you would go after this segment of the audience when there are concerns about the current audience is mind boggling.'"[6]

Safe haven on Facebook? What we used to think of as safe haven for kids was their family home. That haven is now stripped of such status by (you guessed it) FB and other SM platforms that allow kids' social issues at school to relentlessly follow them home. Kids' well-being requires not SM medicine, but just the opposite.

This well-worded statement by Common Sense Media tells the plain unvarnished truth:

> With the growing concerns and pressure around Facebook's business model, the company appears to be doing whatever it takes to identify new revenue streams and short-term corporate profits to impress spooked shareholders. But here's the most important issue: there is absolutely no proof of any meaningful social or educational value of Facebook for children under 13. Indeed, there are very legitimate

> concerns about privacy as well as the impact on the social, emotional, and cognitive development of children. *What Facebook is proposing is similar to the strategies used by Big Tobacco in appealing to young people—try to hook kids early, build your brand, and you have a customer for life.* [Italics mine][7]

A June 2011 *Consumer Reports* "State of the Net" survey "unearthed several disturbing findings about children and Facebook":

> - Of the 20 million minors who actively used Facebook in the past year, 7.5 million—or more than one-third—were younger than 13 and not supposed to be able to use the site.
> - Among young users, more than 5 million were 10 and under, and their accounts were largely unsupervised by their parents.
> - One million children were harassed, threatened, or subjected to other forms of cyberbullying on the site in the past year.
>
> Clearly, using Facebook presents children and their friends and families with safety, security, and privacy risks.[8]

The *Consumer Reports* survey underlines the issue of kids' online safety. What's most troubling is that many parents are not paying attention:

> Parents of kids 10 and younger on Facebook seem to be largely unconcerned. Only 18 percent made their child a Facebook friend, which is the best way to monitor the child. By comparison, 62 percent of parents of 13- to 14-year-olds did so. Only 10 percent of parents of kids 10 and under had frank talks about appropriate online behavior and threats.
>
> Parents of young children might think they are less likely to take risks, some observers say. "It's like an alarm clock goes off for parents

> when their kids turn 13," says Vanessa Van Petten, creator of Radical Parenting, a blog featuring writing by teenagers that aims to improve family relationships. "Parents think their younger kids aren't interested in porn. With a 10-year-old mentality, they're only interested in 10-year-old things."
>
> But those parents would be mistaken. Ten-year-olds need protection from other hazards that might lurk on the Internet, such as links that infect their computer with malware and invitations from strangers, not to mention bullies.[9]

The Internet was not designed for children. Neither was social media. These grown-up domains are accessed by costly devices that children can't afford to buy.

Think about that. And consider again the safety issue.

We can't make the world safe for our kids. A necessary part of growing up is learning to deal with real and imagined dangers. We do, however, have a duty as parents to guide children through a succession of life challenges as best we can. And it is our society's responsibility to call attention to and address large-scale threats to children's wellbeing—especially the new set of dangers the Darkweb holds. We must all protect kids as best we can, especially on that mostly lawless Information Superhighway.

Safety must come first.

Surfing the Net wasn't always as easy as it is now. I remember the mental tenacity it took to use the early computers with their slow, hit-and-miss dial-up Internet connections and frequent glitches. With today's reliable high-speed computing, the vehicles on the Information Superhighway have no trouble starting and roll very smoothly, and younger and younger kids want to drive. And that's what started me on this book. So we can talk about how to find a reasonable way forward in all this.

The medium is the problem. Shiny tech is attractive, personal and fun. Easy online access on a variety of devices is very new, very tantalizing and, with regard to young users, very worrisome. SM shares us in texts and images. It attracts young users who don't know its dangers let alone the impact of shiny tech use on their psyche.

The world is too much with us, Wordsworth wrote. He could not have imagined that it now fits in our hand, we carry it in our pocket.

@crimefighterguy

DARREN LAUR OF the Victoria, BC, police department is not your average @crimefighterguy (his Twitter name), that's for sure. He often speaks at schools, where he informs hundreds (and occasionally thousands) of students at a time about the perils of SM vulnerability. "I'm known to be a white-hatter," Darren says. "I'm what is called a 'good creeper.' I creep for the purposes of education." He socially engineers—manipulates—the profiles of unsuspecting young persons for weeks, not only to gain entry to their social networks, but also to find their homes and steal their personal identity. Then, when he visits their school, he confronts them with what he's discovered—shock therapy that wakes kids up to the harsh realities of the Information Superhighway.

According to a TV news report, Darren "creeped" a middle school in Port Alberni, BC, and made 20 new "friends" (age 11 to 15) in less than 30 minutes.[10] That's typical of all the schools he's presented at in British Columbia. The kids are shocked to learn their new friend isn't real. He doesn't "out" them or embarrass them in front of their friends. Darren has presented to 112,000 students in BC, Saskatchewan and Washington State in the past 24 months, using the same FB profile the entire time, and no one has "outed" him.

> Like it or not, kids are living, eating, sleeping this digital world... We now know that colleges and universities are social engineering students' digital dossiers to say, "Are you the type of student I want coming to my college or university? Are you the type of student I want to hire for a summer job?"[11]

Constable Laur is shedding light on the fact that SM is unforgiving: whatever is posted, whether it's a message, image, link or video, is, from that point on, public or, at the very least, searchable. "One of the things our youth don't understand about the technology is that they believe if their privacy settings are up, the stuff they're posting won't go public, and that's completely false. Anything you post online, no matter what your privacy settings, is public, it's permanent and it's searchable by anybody."[12]

Laur attended an Internet safety talk I hosted on Salt Spring Island as part of the Speaker Series of the Centre for Child Honouring. With our guest speaker, Red Hood Project co-founder Sandy Garossino, we had a lively discussion on many aspects of youth Internet safety, and Darren was an informative participant.

> Kids are digital citizens. Most adults are digital immigrants; they really don't get what's going on in this space...The Internet is going to have its own language, and if you don't speak that language you won't be able to communicate with your kids.[13]

He's right. Already, terms such as *sexting, identity theft, cyberbullying, digital dossiers* are common in a Net culture that may become the norm for these kids. Yet it's not easy to keep up with the evolving SM terminology.

Teen Sharing

FOR A CURRENT take on how social media plays out among high schoolers, I asked Eliza, a dear friend in my community who attends our local high school, for her thoughts. The conversation went like this:

What would happen if you weren't on FB?
I'd lose almost my whole social life, because I wouldn't be included in all the events going on, I wouldn't be invited to the parties you're invited to on FB. I wouldn't be able to comment on photos, to have my photos "liked." People wouldn't see pictures of me. They wouldn't...I'd be off the grid.

Is it like a club?
Yeah, it's like our whole high school online.

How do you feel about that—do you wish it were different?
Yes. I wish that it were more valued to go out and meet people, because I think lots of people have become awkward in person. And they're so comfortable saying things online. And when it comes to really interacting with someone, a lot of people have challenges with that, and that's so sad.

For someone like me, FB is really addicting. I'm on it now and probably gonna sit here even if I wanted to do something else. There are too many interesting things to look at, or addictive things to do.

Are there people at school who conscientiously don't do FB...they just don't like it, or can't afford it...?
No. Well, there's this one girl who, I was really surprised, didn't have FB and, I think, because she wasn't allowed. Eventually she got it, and I'm pretty sure she's more popular now that people can see her pictures.

So looking at the pictures is part of the popularity?
Definitely.

Although people can show you pictures some other way.
Yeah, but it wouldn't happen easily, and the cute guy you have on FB wouldn't see it.

So, for her social ease, it's almost like FB is a must?
Definitely.

Sure, my baby boomer mind was thinking, "We didn't have this in my day, and we did just fine." Maybe that's not the point.

Although this is where I'll tell you what a communications professional (mid-50s, I'd guess) said to me recently. He said that with SM, a teen entering the first year of high school gets the social lay of the land in a few days or, at the most, a few weeks. What took us *several months* when we were in high school—by face-to-face interaction and through a process of time shared and social groups experienced over those months—now seems to happen almost instantly, and almost all of the impressions are made and shared quickly on Facebook, with all the social distortions possible in that hyper-speed way of texting.

Then again, maybe my boomer thought has some relevance. The *compulsive* sharing of images and texts, what's so great about that? Yeah. Way cool.

A Mother's Concern

IN TORONTO, I spoke with a tech-savvy "mommy blogger" (whom I met via Twitter) about SM safety. She was clearly worried. Tracie Wagman said her 10-year-old daughter, Maya, is not allowed to be on FB, even though all her friends are.

> It's shocking to me how many kids are on social media. Many parents don't really know how to use it or what their kids are doing. And the privacy settings: even myself, who is in the industry, has a hard time keeping up with the changes the companies are making and monitoring what's going on. What scares me is that the kids don't understand it so well, and they hide behind the platforms in order to talk about other peers...do the cyberbullying. To keep on top of it, a parent has to be vigilant, and it's *very* difficult. I can barely do it.

If this concerned, aware and motivated parent feels it's hard to cope with the responsibilities of monitoring SM safety for her kids, how will other parents manage?

> In the case of FB, they make changes all the time, and I can't keep track of their settings. How can parents keep up with that and understand? What scares me about social media, what I talk about with other parents, is when the kids start sending pictures of themselves back and forth, as young as grade seven. They don't understand that forwarding or sharing provocative photos of young girls is a criminal offense under child pornography laws.

Tracie believes that "parents should be their kids' friends on FB and they should have the passwords and be monitoring their pages." Like many parents, she also thinks that kids' devices should be kept out of their rooms at night, say, in the kitchen. Responding to my concern about a home where the kids' SM behaviour is always under surveillance, she said, "You want your kids to have a fair amount of freedom. You could have a rule of once a week you'll check, or it may depend on the child. You may have to be more vigilant if you have a tech-savvy child rather than not." I asked Tracie a few more questions:

> *Shiny tech gadgetry is so easy to use, kids feel empowered by a touch of*

the screen. The iPad (or tablet) is a marvel of engineering! Has parenting become exponentially more challenging because of the proliferation of these devices?
I do think so, I think it's become more challenging. Everybody's got them and all their friends too. Peer pressure's not changing, but it's changed in terms of what they're pressured to do. It would be really hard for me to keep Maya off of FB until 16 if every one of her friends were on it and that's how they were communicating with each other. And now they are, they're all texting.

Do you think there's a climate of hyper-anxiety about kids having cellphones to keep in touch with their parents all the time?
There's a fear, some of it from the media. Parents need to learn to let go, to teach their kids independence. Parents don't do that as much—God forbid your child walked two blocks alone. It sets your children up for failure later, for making their own decisions. A cyber expert told me he can find out just about anything he wants: what school you go to, where you live. On Google Maps he can see the doors and windows in your house.

This is why Red Hood Project says that social media providers have the responsibility to curtail this "too much info."
I like Red Hood Project, I like it a lot. I scared my daughter so much, about FB and predators out there, that she actually didn't want to go on it. Maybe I overdid it, but to be honest, I don't know if I could. She should be scared. She definitely lets her friends know she's not on it.

Are you concerned with cellphones and microwaves, the impact on health?
Yes, I've been working on this. It's actually very scary. I've been talking to a scientist who says the wireless tech is dangerous. In our house, we wired everything. We don't even have a cordless phone anymore.

I'll come back to this last point later in Part 1.

Safety by Design

THOSE SHINY TECHNOLOGIES that offer useful services—smartphones, tablets and others—are the manifestation of designed intentions. When they were first developed, no one thought about the implications for privacy. But now that individual privacy and young user safety concerns are paramount throughout the world in this digital age, it's time for hardware and software developers to introduce systemic changes: to design products intended to protect privacy and assure safety.

The enormous online data tracking of SM is a security concern for all users. A CNN opinion piece put it bluntly:

> The Internet is a surveillance state. Whether we admit it to ourselves or not, and whether we like it or not, we're being tracked all the time. Google tracks us, both on its pages and on other pages it has access to. Facebook does the same; it even tracks non-Facebook users. Apple tracks us on our iPhones and iPads. One reporter used a tool called Collusion to track who was tracking him; 105 companies tracked his Internet use during one 36-hour period.
>
> Increasingly, what we do on the Internet is being combined with other data about us...Everything we do now involves computers, and computers produce data as a natural by-product. Everything is now being saved and correlated, and many big-data companies make money by building up intimate profiles of our lives from a variety of sources.
>
> Facebook, for example, correlates your online behavior with your purchasing habits offline. And there's more. There's location data from your cellphone, there's a record of your movements from closed-circuit TVs.

> This is ubiquitous surveillance: All of us being watched, all the time, and that data being stored forever. This is what a surveillance state looks like, and it's efficient beyond the wildest dreams of George Orwell.[14]

This most unsavoury situation has happened with our complicity, if not our outright consent.

The so-called democratization of information bites democracy itself. Pun intended, but nobody's laughing—and if they are, it's to keep from crying. In the United States, the National Defense Authorization Act and other measures since 9/11 have significantly curtailed individual freedoms. In a shocking spectacle in Canada in 2010, during the G20 Summit held in Toronto, with its massive security budget of nearly $1 billion, over 1,000 demonstrators were arrested simply for expressing dissent, including many bystanders. Internet surveillance adds to (and perhaps enables) the previously unthinkable spying on citizens who have every right to privacy and security.

"Privacy by Design" (PbD) is the brainchild of Dr Ann Cavoukian, an internationally renowned privacy expert who champions privacy as an important value to protect proactively, rather than something to tend to later.[15] In 2010, an international assembly of privacy commissioners and data protection authorities was unanimous in its resolution to recognize PbD as an "an essential component of fundamental privacy protection" and to "encourage the adoption of Privacy by Design's Foundational Principles...as guidance to establishing privacy as an organization's default mode of operation."[16] Those Foundational Principles are:

- Proactive not Reactive; Preventative not Remedial
- Privacy as the Default
- Privacy Embedded into Design

- Full Functionality: Positive-Sum, not Zero-Sum
- End-to-End Lifecycle Protection
- Visibility and Transparency
- Respect for User Privacy

Dr Cavoukian is Information and Privacy Commissioner for the province of Ontario and also chairs the advisory committee of the Identity, Privacy and Security Initiative (IPSI) at the University of Toronto, which "is dedicated to developing new approaches to security that maintain the privacy, freedom and safety of the individual and the broader community."[17] Dr George Tomko, IPSI's expert-in-residence for cognitive agent development, has developed a smart tech method that embodies PbD:

> Imagine if your personal data could protect itself? Enter "SmartData." SmartData empowers personal data by wrapping it in a "cloak of intelligence" such that it now becomes the individual's virtual proxy in cyberspace, controlling the release of one's data, in accordance with the user's preferences.
>
> ...An entirely new form of Artificial Intelligence—bottom-up, not top-down—this agent will proactively build-in privacy and security, right from the outset, so that nothing is treated as an afterthought. This is the embodiment of Privacy by Design: embedding a foundation of control and trust within the technology itself as the first line of defense, and incorporating the privacy principles of purpose specification, consent, security, and use limitation.[18]

Sounds impressive, though it remains to be seen exactly how this will work. IPSI's elaborate proposal for funding for SmartData has more scientific detail than I can reference here, but if there's no downside, using smart tech to protect online privacy may be just what the privacy doctor ordered.

If we can have privacy by intention—by design—why not safety? Red Hood Project seeks a "safety by design" solution to the cyber security problem for young users. We advocate for systemic change in these areas:

- Age verification
- Disabled location and web browser tracking
- Default privacy settings
- Firewall protection for children's data online

As mentioned earlier, Red Hood insists that social media corporations have an obligation to provide advanced security protections that safeguard children from known threats. To learn more about how we can all hold the SM industry accountable in establishing safety standards that protect our kids, please see Appendix B.

Cellphone Safe?

THE SOCIAL AND emotional risks of SM use go hand in hand with the potential physiological and developmental risks associated with the wireless tech devices used by the young.

In February 2013, a pediatric neurologist at Harvard, Dr Martha Herbert, sent a letter to the Los Angeles Unified School District to caution the district against pursuing its plan to equip all its schools with WiFi. Dr Herbert has done extensive research and clinical work on neurodevelopmental disorders, and brain development and function. She is concerned about the effects of wireless technology:

> Current technologies were designed and promulgated without taking account of biological impacts other than thermal impacts. We now know that there are a large array of impacts that have nothing to do

> with the heating of tissue. The claim from wifi proponents that the only concern is thermal impacts is now definitively outdated scientifically.
>
> EMF/RFR [electromagnetic fields/radiofrequency radiation] from wifi and cell towers can exert a disorganizing effect on the ability to learn and remember, and can also be destabilizing to immune and metabolic function. This will make it harder for some children to learn, particularly those who are already having problems in the first place.
>
> Powerful industrial entities have a vested interest in leading the public to believe that EMF/RFR, which we cannot see, taste or touch, is harmless, but this is not true. *Please do the right and precautionary thing for our children.* [Italics mine]
>
> I urge you to step back from your intention to go wifi in the LAUSD, and instead opt for wired technologies, particularly for those sub-populations that are most sensitive. It will be easier for you to make a healthier decision now than to undo a misguided decision later.[19]

A month later, the American Academy of Environmental Medicine (AAEM) also wrote to the Los Angeles Unified School District:

> To install this system in Los Angeles risks a widespread public health question that the medical system is not yet prepared to answer.
>
> ...While technicians and sales staff argue about the validity of the dangers posed by cell towers, cellphones, WiFi and other forms of wireless radiation, it is the doctors who must deal with the fall out. Until we, as doctors, can determine why some of our patients become debilitatingly sick from WiFi and other microwave communications, while others do not, we implore you not to take such a known risk with the health of so many children who have entrusted you to keep them safe while at school.[20]

The precautionary principle advocated by Martha Herbert and the AAEM is precisely what pediatrician Dr Philip Landrigan proposed in his chapter on emerging technologies for the American Academy of Pediatrics' book *Pediatric Environmental Health*. Dr Landrigan, head of the Children's Environmental Health Center at the Mt Sinai Medical Center in New York, called for "a new child-protective national strategy in the US for prudent stewardship of emerging technologies and new chemicals":

> This new framework needs to be based on prudence and precaution. It must be designed explicitly to protect children. It must overturn the dangerous and outdated assumption that new technologies pose no risk until they have been proven beyond all doubt to cause harm.
>
> The Precautionary Principle needs to be the bedrock of this new national framework. The key element of the precautionary principle is that it provides justification for acting in the face of uncertainty. It is a tool for acting on the basis of early warnings. Under the precautionary principle, the burden of proof is shifted. New technologies are no longer presumed safe. Instead, safety must be documented.[21]

Dr Landrigan chaired the National Academy of Sciences Committee on Pesticides in the Diets of Infants and Children, which affirmed that "children are not little adults," and that the unique vulnerabilities of a young child's developing body must be the standard for setting lower risk levels for exposure to toxic chemicals as compared to a fully developed adult body.[22]

This standard and the precautionary principle are key points for all aspects of SM and shiny tech, and I have emphasized them in my writings, both in the anthology *Child Honouring* and in essays. We must reverse the onus of proof of safety for new technologies from user to manufacturer, whether that's safety for physical health or for mental and emotional health.

Recommendations for caution come from many other sources.

Dr Sanjay Gupta, CNN's medical commentator, has reported that, although children's brains are far more vulnerable to the microwave radiation from cellphones, the research on safe microwave limits is based on adult use of cellphones. And information on safe limits for children won't be conclusive for some time, Dr Gupta says, possibly 30 years or more.[23]

Dr Keith Black, chair of neurosurgery and neuroscience at Cedar Sinai Medical Centre in Los Angeles, confirms that the amount of radiation absorbed by a child's brain is much higher than the amount absorbed by the adult brain. As a result, he says:

> We should be cautious with how we allow our children to use a cellphone. They're going to be the ones not only using it at a much younger age, but using it over a much longer duration...
>
> I use a cellphone, but I always use it either on speaker mode or use it with an earpiece or text. I don't put it next to my brain...So, if you want to take precautions, at least you're aware that your cellphone is not necessarily a safe device.[24]

Dr David Carpenter, director of the Institute for Health and the Environment at the School of Public Health, University at Albany, SUNY, is outspoken on the subject of WiFi safety:

> Based on existing science, many public health experts believe, myself included, that it is possible we will face an epidemic of cancers in the future resulting from uncontrolled use of cell phones and increased population exposure to WI-FI and other wireless devices. Thus it is important that all of us, and especially children, restrict our use of cell phones, and limit exposure to background levels of WI-FI.[25]

Further, Dr Carpenter supports the right of personal choice in relation to health risks associated with so-called smart meter installations for hydro use, stating, "It should be up to each individual to identify whether or not they want to be continuously exposed 24/7 to elevated levels of radiofrequency radiation."[26] This is a matter of personal interest to me. In my home province of British Columbia, the provincial hydro utility has trampled on people's right to decide whether radiofrequency radiation might enter their home. I'm one of thousands who refuse the anti-democratic privacy intrusion and related health risks of a wireless device for hydro meter reading.

Around the world, organizations, cities and governments are expressing concern and taking precautionary actions, as outlined in an 18-minute Australian video, *WiFi in Schools—The Facts*, which notes the following examples, among others:

- The Council of Europe has said that "the limits on exposure to electromagnetic fields...set for the general public are obsolete" and has called for stricter exposure limits for all equipment that emits electromagnetic waves. It has also called for a ban on WiFi use in schools and recommends wired Internet connections in schools.
- Several schools in England and France have dismantled their WiFi systems and reverted to a wired system due to concerns raised by parents and teachers.
- The French national library, along with other libraries and some universities, have removed all WiFi networks...The Bavarian Parliament has recommended that no schools in the province use wireless. The Frankfurt city government has said that it would not install WiFi in its schools until it has been proven to be harmless. The German government recommends against installation of WiFi in schools, [and recommends] the removal of cordless phones, and to use cabled connections rather than WiFi and Bluetooth.
- In 2008 the Russian Radiation Protection Committee gave a warning about the serious and irreparable consequences of electromagnetic radiation [EMR], especially for children. They increased

this warning again in 2011 and recommended that WiFi not be used in schools.

- In Austria, the Austrian Medical Association has pressed for a ban of WiFi in schools. The Swiss government has issued caution in regard to wireless radiation emitted by [such devices as] baby monitors, cellphones...etc.
- In May 2011, the World Health Organization classified radiofrequency electromagnetic radiation as possible human carcinogens.[27]

The video concludes:

> When it comes to long-term health risks, governments don't always take swift actions or a precautionary approach. This was the case with smoking and asbestos...Authorities like the European Parliament and the European Environmental Agency believe that there is already sufficient scientific evidence for governments to take an immediate precautionary approach, especially to protect children who are most vulnerable. They state that "waiting for high levels of scientific and clinical proof can lead to very high health and economic costs as was the case in the past with asbestos, leaded petrol and tobacco. However, ignoring the early warning could be much worse, as EMR affects everybody."[28]

Electro-hypersensitivity, also known as electromagnetic hypersensitivity (EHS), is a condition in which people have debilitating reactions to being around wireless technologies. Symptoms include headaches, insomnia, dizziness, heart palpitations and reduced cognitive function (concentration, memory). In some cases, people with EHS have to move to a region with little or no microwave radiation. Nowadays, such places seem to be few and far between.

The formative physiology of the young child deserves special consideration. For as the child goes, so goes society. Formative—it's a word for everyone to understand. For what's forming in early months and first years is not just the physical body but also a person's sense of self. Both of these are the very basis for a lifetime of health outcomes.

Be cautious. Don't get your kids a mobile until the teen years. Save money, avoid their use of a distractive device and protect their health. At least ensure they understand the need to hold it away from their head or, better yet, to use it with an earpiece or with the speakerphone feature. Model this good behaviour yourself.

Internet Hurting Kids?

WE SIMPLY DO not know—cannot know—whether the digital revolution that has overtaken our species is ultimately in our best interest. Not enough time has elapsed for studies to show clear and lasting benefits of the digital medicine.

In a 2012 article "Is the Internet Hurting Children?" Chelsea Clinton and co-author Jim Steyer ask a most important question:

> *What are the real effects of all this on the huge segment of the population most affected by social media themselves: our children and our teens?*
>
> The explosive growth of social media, smartphones and digital devices is transforming our kids' lives, in school and at home. Research tells us that even the youngest of our children are migrating online, using tablets and smartphones, downloading apps. Consumer Reports reported last year that more than 7.5 million American kids under the age of 13 have joined Facebook, which technically requires users to be 13 years old to open an account. *No one has any idea of what all of this media and technology use will mean for our kids as they grow up.* [Italics mine][29]

That digital media is pervasive among kids is easy to see. In the United States, by the time they are 5 years old, more than half the kids interact regularly with a computing device, and by 8 years a great many are playing video games. Clinton and Steyer point out that by the time kids reach middle school, they spend less time with teachers and parents than they do with media. They go on to say:

> Our new world of digital immersion and multitasking has affected everything from our thought processes and work habits to our capacity for linear thinking and how we feel about ourselves, our friends and even strangers. And it has all happened virtually overnight.[30]

Clinton and Steyer note that "the promise of digital media to transform our lives in positive ways is enormous," but this optimism is predicated on a key condition.

> *If managed well* [italics mine], technology can improve our schools and education, deepen social connectedness, expand civic engagement and even help advance our democracy.[31]

The article closes with a clear call for changes in teaching, behaviour and laws to optimize the Lightweb by curbing the Darkweb:

> We need legislation, educational efforts and norms that reflect 21st-century realities to maximize the opportunities and minimize the risks for our kids. Only then will we be able to give them the safe, healthy childhood and adolescence they deserve.[32]

I agree. We will indeed need legislation, and soon. Without that, it's hard to imagine how we'll get the needed reforms to decisively move the risk-benefit ratio in favour of the Lightweb.

• • •

In his book *The Net Delusion*, Evgeny Morozov cuts to the heart of the digital revolution's "carte blanche" with our lives.

> The recognition of the revolutionary nature of a technology is a poor excuse not to regulate it. Smart regulation, if anything, is a first sign that society is serious about the technology in question and believes that it is here to stay; that it is eager to think through the consequences; and that it wants to find ways to unleash and harvest its revolutionary potential. No society has ever got such regulatory frameworks right by looking only at technology's bright sides and refusing to investigate how its uses may also produce effects harmful to society.[33]

We are humans—emotionally functioning biological beings who depend on the biosphere for our existence. As intelligent animals, we are equipped with a brain of dazzling capabilities that allows us to feel our way in the world, wonder and make meaning, and dream of better tomorrows.

Being human involves obedience to empathy and compassion, our higher nature. We stand up to injustice, we defend our young. We resist unhealthy enculturation. We honour community by standing guard for democracy. We rally the courage of nonviolence.

"First, do no harm" can be a precautionary mantra for our times: an oath physicians take that each one of us must embrace. And with first years being the most vulnerable to any harm, the word "first" is doubly significant, pertaining to formative "first years" experience for the impressionable physiology of infants. The growing brain's plasticity in adolescence and in much later years means that we'd be wise to use best practices in keeping our young, and ourselves, in a healthy way.

Ensuring privacy and security for all who use social media is of paramount importance. The safety of young users is a primary reason to reform social media without delay.

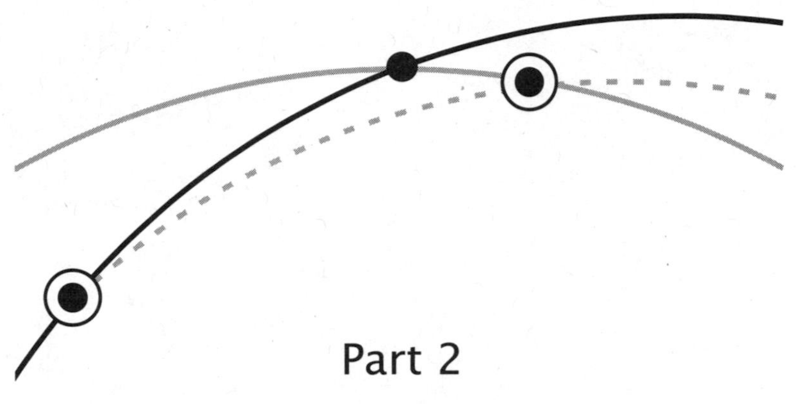

Part 2

INTELLIGENCE

Ain't nothin' like the real thing baby, ain't nothin' like the real thing.
~ Marvin Gaye and Tammi Terrell

Never have we more needed to keep our eye on the real.
Our tools must help us accomplish that; and if they don't,
we have to reshape what we have made.
~ Sherry Turkle

A VAST SOCIOLOGICAL experiment is underway. For the first time, tweens and teens live in two worlds, real and virtual, in homes where their parents themselves spend a lot of family time online. The kids want to mimic what they see adults do—to flash the new electric gear.

2013 feels like a very different world than 2004, the start-up year of Facebook. Kids are growing up with the new electricity. It surrounds them, it's with them, it's inside them. They've got the whole world in their hands: wireless connection to information, people and places. They're drawn to cruise the facsimile world before they learn to dance with the real world. They connect virtually online before learning the art of personal interaction. They text before cultivating the art of human conversation.

The first reason to reform social media is safety. The second reason, intelligence, is directly related to the first. If the young of our species cannot be safe to develop their intelligence using the most popular and seductive technological invention, then we should certainly rethink its value and its place in our lives. Let us now consider the intelligence at play in and impacted by the digital world.

A Precious Gift

HUMAN INTELLIGENCE IS a precious gift of evolution. Through millennia our species has exercised its mental prowess, courageous heart and indomitable spirit. Darwin's notes on the "moral sensitivity" of our species recognized the innately empathic animal that we are, biologically social and caring, our most endearing quality.[1]

Digital technology's promise is a connected global village that inspires virtuous changes in our species' conduct. That's quite a vision, one against which current practices must be examined. A big-picture view of what we call society will help us fully grasp the global SM experiment—what drives it, what drives us, what drives society. All our human impulses, whether basic drives of sex and survival or our higher aspirations, are framed by the cultural values we live by. What is it that most families are after? What do the children need so they can thrive?

The Rolling Stones' lyrics are far less contentious than referencing Karl Marx on the subject of wants vs needs: "You can't always get what you want," the Stones sing, but sometimes "you get what you need." We all know that needs and wants are very different. But while the former may claim first dibs, wants aren't frivolous; they fire our imagination, dreams and aspirations.

Abraham Maslow's theory of a Hierarchy of Needs outlined a sequential fulfillment of needs: from necessities for basic survival (love, shelter, safety) to growth needs that include self-esteem, realizing one's potential and becoming, as he put it, self-actualized.[2] Critics of this theory had a point: it's not as if our wants can wait until our needs are met. Nor do those whose basic needs are unfulfilled have less glorious wants. Striving is a great creator of art and of means.

I've often thought that had Maslow lived longer, his Hierarchy of Needs theory might have evolved into a Holarchy of Needs, Rights and Responsibilities. I'm fond of holarchy and its "systems nested within systems" holism, as compared to hierarchy's linear ascension. I'd have loved to chat with him about this. For one thing, the holarchy idea would include rights and responsibilities, which, to my mind, go together. Our individual rights exist in community, and that relational context involves our responsibilities to one another.

What's more, in considering the rights of children (expressed in the UN's Convention on the Rights of the Child[3]), we can focus on the *universal* needs of the young child whose rights are indeed needs—developmentally speaking—because they are *irreducible* needs. And if we share a strong sense of community, affirming and protecting their rights are indeed our responsibilities.

Unhealthy Enculturation

FROM ABRAHAM MASLOW'S extraordinary understanding of human nature comes this gem: healthy individuation requires resisting unhealthy enculturation. This is something I've taken to heart. The point in personal growth and emotional healing work is not to become well-adjusted to an unhealthy culture. The goal, rather, is to become whole, with a mature set of values with which to live and connect. The goal is wholeness, maturation.

There are many signs of unhealthy culture in a civilization that currently seems stuck in short-termism, like a juvenile refusing to grow up, needing intervention. One clear sign is a predatory commercial culture and its willful exploitation of the young. Culture as bully. It's our duty to resist it, to change it, to orient societal priorities towards life-affirming values and to oppose life-destroying practices.

Resistance to unhealthy culture is not an option, it's our duty.

As I prepped for this book, researching the pros and cons of digital culture, a number of books and articles and YouTube talks by their authors caught my attention. Years ago I'd read Internet-touting books such as *Growing Up Digital: The Rise of the Net Generation*, by InfoTech enthusiast Don Tapscott, and I was aware of the work of digital utopians such as Nicholas Negroponte and Ray Kurzweil. Now I needed to hear other voices, the voices of caution.

So, of course, I searched Amazon.com and found many helpful books.

First, I was intrigued and entranced by *Alone Together,* a book by MIT professor Sherry Turkle, who has worked for decades studying people's complex interactions with computers. Regarding the currently "always connected" state of young SM users, Turkle rightly cautions that children "will only know how to be lonely" if they are not taught how to be alone. "For adult and child, having gotten into the habit of constant connection, we risk losing our capacity for the kind of solitude that energizes and restores."[4]

Then I read Nicholas Carr's Pulitzer-nominated book *The Shallows: What the Internet Is Doing to Our Brains.* Carr recognizes the Internet's numerous benefits and yet sounds practical alarms about skills, such as deep reading and comprehension, that may be lost in Net immersion: "The strip mining of 'relevant content' replaces the slow excavation of meaning."[5] He's outspoken on the Internet's impact on the brain: "With the exception of alphabets and number systems, the Net may well be the most powerful and mind-altering technology that has ever come into general use."[6]

The Digital Divide, a 2011 anthology edited by Mark Bauerlein, offers a diversity of views on the digital revolution, from enthusiasts and critics alike. In one splendid book, articles both recently written and from the mid-1990s provide an informative look into the Internet's design, promise and delivery.[7]

But the more digital critique I heard and read, the more I wondered why the InfoTech cheerleaders were so gung ho about it without sufficient cautions.

I can understand the enthusiasts' early excitement. Who wouldn't have got buzzed about digital revolution, "wiring the global brain" and other such lofty ideas!

Yet you can hardly wire the global brain if in the process you fry the real brain, especially the very young brain, born and growing in the real world.

Brain Storms

THAT THE PREVALENCE of the Internet is changing the brains of users is coming to be understood. From the impact of the visual screen on infant brains to digital media's distractive influence on adolescent behaviour, the rapid changes in human habits from a prolonged time spent in "virtuality" are very real. Consider, then, the effect of digital technology on *formative* intelligence and its seat in the dazzling human brain. Our brain.

Dr Dimitri Christakis is a pediatrician and researcher at Seattle Children's Hospital. In an engaging TEDxRainier presentation, Dr Christakis tells us that by the age of 2, a newborn's brain triples in size—a growth spurt found only in this early time of life.

> We're actually born with a lifetime supply of brain cells and neurons. That's not what actually grows. It's the connections between those brain cells, what we call synapses, that account for that brain growth. And those synapses form based on early experiences...The mind is fine-tuned to the world that babies inhabit.[8]

Dr Christakis adds that the newborn brain has 2,500 synapses [per neuron], and that number grows to 15,000 by age 3. Our brains grow in relationships, with people and with our surroundings. Love grows brains, as Roots of Empathy founder Mary Gordon is fond of saying. We are innately primed to connect; in fact, we can't help it. What technology we encounter in those early months—in particular, electronic visual media—affects the kinds of neural connections made in our brain, as well as our capacity for human connection. Dr Christakis argues:

> We are technologizing childhood today in a way that is unprecedented. In 1970, the average age at which children began to watch television regularly was 4 years...Today, based on research we've done, it's 4 months. It's not just how early they watch but how much they watch. The typical child, before the age of 5, is watching about four and a half hours of TV a day. That represents as much as 40 percent of their waking hours.

Based on his research, Dr Christakis has developed the "overstimulation hypothesis," which suggests that "prolonged exposure to this rapid image change [of TV programs] during this critical window of brain development would precondition the mind to expect high levels of input, and that would lead to inattention in later life." In other words, each hour of TV stimulation per day at the start of life means the chance these children will have problems paying attention later on is increased by 10 percent. But here's the good news about cognitive stimulation: Dr Christakis reminds us that each hour parents spend reading to children, taking them to a museum, singing to them reduces the likelihood of inattention in later years by 30 percent.

Any policy maker with this kind of information might wonder why as a society we're not doing all we can to make early experience an affirming time for every single child in our communities. As Dr Christakis concludes:

> We need more real-time play today and less fast-paced media, particularly for young children...If we change the beginning of the story, we change the whole story.[9]

That last line bears repeating. Memorize it. Post it on your laptop. Put it on your fridge: "If we change the beginning of the story, we change the whole story."

Stuart Shanker, Distinguished Research Professor of Philosophy and Psychology at York University, makes a similar point about how early experiences determine "how effectively and efficiently a child deals with stress and recovers":

> Human babies are [born] premature, their brains at birth are a quarter of adult brain size...At the moment of birth the brain explodes...700 synapses form every single second for the first year of life... It's adapting to its environment, and unfortunately if that environment is a highly stressful environment...it's setting off a hair-trigger stress response...
>
> By the age of six and a half, 95 percent of the brain's growth has now been completed...The brain of a 7-year-old is very stable...All the core systems—language, reflective thinking—these have all become highly entrenched...
>
> There's a very interesting reason for this. Children cannot regulate themselves; they need their parents or an adult to regulate them. And it is by being regulated that a child develops the ability to self-regulate.
>
> The systems that I just mentioned that are exploding after birth... get wired in these back-and-forth interactions with your parents... The parts of the brain that are exploding learn how to do this for themselves and the kid goes on to do it.[10]

This is why child development professionals have been saying, in every way they can, that it's the time *before* a child enters formal learning that shapes lifelong outcomes. It's what I've been emphasizing in my Child Honouring presentations at conferences and universities, and it's what David Elkind has also pointed out about the benefits of raising unhurried children: they are grounded and grow to be resourceful.[11]

If a nascent brain experiences a lot of negative stimulation, it's preconditioned for stress in later life. Shanker says we're seeing this now, "signs of excessive adrenaline, signs of excessive stress" in the lives of teenagers and even younger children. He goes on to say:

> The stressors could be environmental: the stress of living in the city, of noise, of light. It could be social: the stress of a family that's overstressed. It can be emotional; we divide emotions into two categories: positive and negative. Negative emotions—fear, anger, sadness, frustration, anxiety—burn enormous amounts of energy. And paradoxically, positive emotions release neurochemicals which create energy. Parents don't understand this, even well-meaning parents.[12]

The result is "kids who are not mentally ill, but neither are they mentally healthy," Shanker says. When it comes to young people and screen time, much depends on social context, age and content. Yet given what we know about the sedentary habits of kids and the hyper-violent and hyper-sexual pop culture producing much of what they consume onscreen, we need to be aware of the costs incurred:

> For a teen, it is a stressor not being involved with other kids face to face. That's a huge stressor. We know categorically that television and video games are...physiological stressors. Just think about it this way...The brain consumes 20 percent of the body's energy, the visual system consumes 65 percent of the brain's energy. So by spending four hours a day in front of a TV and another 3 hours a day in front of a computer...these systems that are designed to keep them locked on the screen, are a huge metabolic cost.

Shanker cites a related problem, which is the lack of sufficient exercise teens and younger children get when they are seated in front of a screen for long periods of time. Exercise is a natural self-regulator.

The other thing that affects one's capacity for self-regulation is chronic sleep loss.

> We have a generation of teenagers who are two hours under-slept, and a generation of children who are two hours under-slept. All of our kids are under-slept, even our babies are under-slept, compared to just a decade ago.[13]

An under-slept society whose kids spend seven hours a day in front of screens does not have the makings of a healthy culture. (And while it's true that book reading is also a sedentary endeavour, it is a very different experience than being online, more conducive to imaginative stirrings and deep reflection.)

Nicholas Carr addresses the issue of Net dependence and addiction in *The Shallows:* "The Net delivers precisely the kind of sensory and cognitive stimuli—repetitive, intensive, interactive, addictive—that have been shown to result in strong and rapid alterations in brain circuits and functions."[14] In other words, use of social media offers that same repetitive, addictive, dopamine-inducing "reward" and expectation that keeps users hooked.

When I asked Annie Leonard, a mother in California, if the Internet age complicates parenting her daughter, Dewi, she told me:

> Absolutely. SM has added to the challenges of parenting—in many ways. It is one more thing that keeps the kids from going outdoors, reading a book, playing a board game or doing other healthy, curiosity-cultivating activities. Also, pre-teens do stupid stuff. As Jill Bolte Taylor explains so well, the teenage brain isn't developed in the good-judgment-making department. With today's social media the stupid stuff kids do is photographed and posted for the whole world to see. They don't understand the implications of living out silly adolescent stuff on an internationally visible platform.

My daughter is smart, engaged, an avid book reader and a critical thinker—and still I find myself having to tell her that she needs to turn off the screen and go to sleep, or remind her that there are no screens at the meal table.

I picked her up at the airport Sunday after a weekend she had away, and the first thing she did when getting in my car is grab for my phone to check Facebook. She intellectually understands all the risks and problems, but the combination of having a pre-teen level of judgment and the highly addictive quality of SM results in a constant struggle within herself and sometimes between us.

There are some good things about it too, but I believe the technology is evolving faster than our understanding of it and our cultural norms around it. If it were not so omnipresent, but was an occasional thing they used to share information, it wouldn't be so bad. Dewi uses SM to gain support for her various activities around social justice causes. She is also a serious rock climber and her climbing teammates share training videos and live stream of competitions that are thrilling—and educational—for climbers to watch.

So, in many ways, the issue is limits: there are no boundaries. It is there all the time, in most kids' pockets all day. I have seen rooms full of 13-year-old girls where no one talks to each other but they are sitting in silence texting each other.

Screen Dilemma

BACK IN THE 1980s, media critic Neil Postman took Marshall McLuhan's famous phrase "The medium is the message" and gave it a twist for kids and television: "It's not what they watch, it's that they watch." Postman meant that for little kids, who don't have enough life experience to cognitively make sense of TV imagery, the content is secondary to the experience. He was referring to the overbearing nature of the TV medium's intrusive impact (with prefabricated images) on the infant physiology. A television broadcasting in the living room blurs the adult-child divide by offering moving images that take no skill to watch. Children love Saturday morning cartoons, and *Sesame Street*, in Neil Postman's razor-sharp observation, taught children to love television.[15] Now, shiny tech mobile devices further blur the adult-child divide.

In the 2012 report *Facing the Screen Dilemma: Young Children, Technology and Early Education*, Campaign for a Commercial-Free Childhood and two other organizations concerned about tech's effect on children state, "There's no question that screen technologies are drastically changing the lives of children. As a result, early childhood educators face a complex dilemma."[16] Marie Winn, author of *The Plug-In Drug*, concurs: "The electronic media are so much more pervasive in early childhood. You can find screen devices in cradles, in cribs, in strollers. They are widely used in potty training! The effects on the vulnerable brain are indisputable."[17]

Research shows that "the new technologies haven't displaced television and video in children's lives—they have added to screen time,"[18] escalating an already pressing issue.

Despite the advice of the American Academy of Pediatrics that children under 2 watch no TV, screens increasingly intrude into young lives:

> Media use begins in infancy. On any given day, 29% of babies under the age of 1 are watching TV and videos for an average of about 90 minutes. Twenty-three percent have a television in their bedroom. Time with screens increases rapidly in the early years. Between their first and second birthday, on any given day, 64% of babies and toddlers are watching TV and videos, averaging slightly over 2 hours. Thirty-six percent have a television in their bedroom. Little is known about the amount of time children under 2 currently spend with smartphones

> and tablets, but in 2011 there were three million downloads just of Fisher Price apps for infants and toddlers."[19]

This screen time is at the very start of life, the formative time for the growth of intelligence that colours the whole of a person's experience. We know that it's early years experience that largely shapes the emotional tone of being and outcomes in health, resourcefulness, creativity and productivity for a lifetime. Early social impressions are what connect the growing brain, for better or worse.

> Data vary on screen time for preschoolers. But even the most conservative findings show that children between the ages of 2 and 5 average 2.2 hours per day. Other studies show that preschoolers spend as much as 4.125 to 4.6 hours per day using screen media. As children grow older, screen time increases and they tend to use more than one medium at the same time. Including when they're multi-tasking, 8- to 18-year-olds consume an average of 7 hours and 11 minutes of screen media per day—*an increase of 2.5 hours in just 10 years.* [Italics mine][20]

And with kids using SM at a younger age than we expected, the concern grows: "Even as social networking sites are being marketed to young children, a study by Stanford University researchers has found that girls ages 8 to 12 who are heavy users of social media are less happy and more socially uncomfortable than their peers."[21]

Because young children learn best while outside, with people, and by using their whole bodies in active play and sensory rich environments, the report's conclusion comes as no surprise:

> There's no evidence that screen time is educational for infants and toddlers, and there is some evidence that it may be harmful. Some carefully monitored experience with quality content can benefit children over 3. But what's most important for children is lots of time for

hands-on creative and active play, time in nature, and face-to-face interactions with caring adults. And, regardless of content, excessive screen time harms healthy growth and development.[22]

Parents have told me their own stories of children who too often shun hands-on creative and active play, time in nature, and face-to-face interactions with caring adults:

- A mother takes her son for a violin class at his teacher's home. During the lesson, the teacher's two kids, aged 9 and 7, are both glued to their InfoTech devices.
- A stay-at-home mother posts a photo on Twitter that shows her typing on her laptop (on a desk). Beside her in a high chair sits her 2-year-old, riveted to a game on a small tech device in his hands.
- A teen daughter tries texting a question to her mother from one part of the house to the other. The mother tells her daughter she will not text her in their home—she expects a *conversation* with her daughter, not a text exchange.
- A father says many of his 11-year-old son's friends won't come over to his house because he won't play video games with them.
- A mother tells me about a friend whose 8-year-old son comes home from school and goes to his room to play hours of video games.
- A mother in Ontario says, "Once my kids have jobs, they can buy their own phone. Same with the laptop."

Bathed in Bits?

IN A 1995 PBS interview, Neil Postman talked about cyberspace as being "something very different than co-presence." He also spoke of the basic conflict with new technologies—that something gained also comes with a cost:

> A new technology is a kind of Faustian bargain. It always gives us something important; it also takes away something important. That's been true of the alphabet, the printing press, telegraphy, and right up to the computer.[23]

Postman was openly opposed to the use of personal computers in school:

> Because school, it seems to me, has always been about how to learn as part of a group. School's never been about individualized learning, but about how to be socialized as a citizen and as a human being. We have important rules in school always emphasizing the fact that one is part of a group.[24]

Naturally, our ideas of what constitutes the best school experience are changing. It's hard to imagine that Postman's thinking on education would not have evolved to embrace the part that computer efficiency can play—in research, for example. I also think he'd have championed the need for digital media literacy and digital citizenry as part of the school curriculum. Yet I respect his wariness of the digital seduction.

We used to say that education was the making of a person. Digivangelists would now have you believe that InfoTech is the making of a person. How absurd. You're still the same person, with tech. And yet, InfoTech is so pervasive that its pretense can seem almost real.

Similarly, the digital tech culture says that if you are not connected, you're disconnected—missing out. And if you believe that, the technology may have already re-formed your worldview without your awareness.

How you are connected, to what and to whom all matter greatly to your quality of life, your perceptions and your sense of the social and ecological. Social networking is only one way to connect.

How digital technology is impacting learning is a subject of hot debate. If you don't know just where to hang your hat in this conversation, rest assured you're not alone. Mark Prensky observes:

> Today's students—[kindergarten] through college—represent the first generations to grow up with this new technology. They have spent their entire lives surrounded by and using computers, videogames, digital music players, video cams, cell phones, and all the other toys and tools of the digital age. Today's average college grads have spent less than 5,000 hours of their lives reading, but over 10,000 hours playing video games (not to mention 20,000 hours watching TV). Computer games, email, the Internet, cell phones and instant messaging are integral parts of their lives.[25]

The InfoTech industry pitches its latest gadgets to educators in every way possible. Entire school boards buy tablets for their primary teachers to use. Even kindergarten teachers tell me (to my utter amazement) that they're using a tablet in class. Little kids have the rest of their lives to engage InfoTech, I tell them. Shiny tech devices are easy to use and take little skill to master; it's simply illogical to worry (as many do) that their kids might be left behind.

Parents and teachers: can we take a moment here?

InfoTech is *so easy* that people master it at any age, without prior experience, let alone childhood training. And as we know all too well, InfoTech and its devices are always changing. No need to start young.

Education leaders, consultants and teachers have widely divergent views on what digital technologies (and how much) would be appropriate for kids of different ages. Many EdTech enthusiasts promote digital tech devices as exciting tools to be widely used.

Classroom teachers do worry about SM's intrusion on the awareness and focusing ability of their students. I asked a group of randomly selected teachers to describe their day-to-day experiences.

A seventh grade teacher complains about having to ask kids to remove cellphones from class and put them in their lockers. She says that ongoing bullying issues (on Facebook) require her intervention. She talks about the presence of digital devices at school:

> Students with technology that is not closely monitored often end up being in a state of constant distraction or emotional upset. They feel anxiety when they are away from their phones, iPads, etc. When the technology is close by they are unable to focus in class. When they leave school they are going to a world that is very different than the one that I grew up in. When I went home I had a safe environment to go to where I could leave behind social issues and any distress I felt during the day. My family spent evenings together engaged in positive interactions.
>
> Today, students go home and their issues follow them. Their friends are constantly texting them, they are being bullied on Facebook, their family members are busy on computers, phones, iPads, etc. There is never a break for them away from all of the pressures and angst of being a tween/teen. I wonder about the effect of constant stress on them as they grow and develop and yet I feel powerless to protect them.

And a high school teacher, who may be speaking for most of her profession, responds to the question "Are cellphones a distraction at school?"

> A distraction? YES!!! With younger grades I tell them up front that if they get caught on it during class it will go on my desk. If they get

> caught again it will go to the office and a parent will have to come and get it. With senior classes it is about respect—for the teacher teaching and the classmates presenting. I will call them out on it. And when it is during a[nother] classmate's presentation, marks are deducted from *their* work for being a poor audience member. It is only with really chronic seniors (immature ones) that I would confiscate their phone and put it on my desk.
>
> With all grade levels I bargain with them that I will always wrap up the day's lesson a couple of minutes before the bell, and then they can get caught up on their social life. With some students I also make them leave their phone if they ask to go to the bathroom, as it is used as a tool to "meet up" with friends.

Just as parents face many new challenges at home, teachers are having a tough time managing the new distractions. The teacher quoted above is also a parent and has more to say about the stress generated by a new reality that, 10 years ago, did not exist:

> The seeming addiction to constantly being connected is creating additional stress on teenagers that those of us over 30 (or well beyond) did not have to deal with. I have a 14-year-old daughter and trying to keep her unplugged, and not drawn into constant gossip and drama, is a challenge. One thing I have implemented in my own home (I have a 16-year-old boy, and 11-year-old and 14-year-old girls) is to require them to leave all of their electronics in at the charging station in the kitchen overnight. Even when they have friends sleep over, the iPods, tablets and phones are not in their rooms after a specific time. This ensures that they are focusing on one another and not what is going on elsewhere. It also ensures they don't get drawn into gossip from a gathering they are not at.

School policies are quite varied about how to deal with the Info-

Tech quandary, though we may see the day when, out of necessity, there might be a mandatory regulation—much like seatbelts—for all schools to uphold. Here's another high school teacher talking about the addictive aspect of SM:

> Digital devices are a great help when used appropriately. However, they are also a distraction. Students can be addicted to their devices, unable to resist peeking at text messages on Facebook while in class. I confiscate devices and hold them until the end of class or send them to the VP for repeat offenders as per school policy.

In a delicious irony, the *New York Times* reported on Silicon Valley tech execs who send their kids to tech-free schools:

> The chief technology officer of eBay sends his children to a nine-classroom school here. So do employees of Silicon Valley giants like Google, Apple, Yahoo and Hewlett-Packard.
>
> But the school's chief teaching tools are anything but high-tech: pens and paper, knitting needles and, occasionally, mud. Not a computer to be found. No screens at all. They are not allowed in the classroom, and the school even frowns on their use at home.
>
> Schools nationwide have rushed to supply their classrooms with computers, and many policy makers say it is foolish to do otherwise. But the contrarian point of view can be found at the epicenter of the tech economy, where some parents and educators have a message: computers and schools don't mix.
>
> This is the Waldorf School of the Peninsula, one of around 160 Waldorf schools in the country that subscribe to a teaching philosophy focused on physical activity and learning through creative, hands-on tasks. Those who endorse this approach say computers inhibit creative thinking, movement, human interaction and attention spans.[26]

Interesting to note the use of the word "contrarian" to describe a perspective different from the InfoTech evangelism.

> "I fundamentally reject the notion you need technology aids in grammar school," said Alan Eagle, 50, whose daughter, Andie, is one of the 196 children at the Waldorf elementary school; his son William, 13, is at the nearby middle school. "The idea that an app on an iPad can better teach my kids to read or do arithmetic, that's ridiculous."
>
> Mr. Eagle knows a bit about technology. He holds a computer science degree from Dartmouth and works in executive communications at Google, where he has written speeches for the chairman, Eric E. Schmidt.

You don't have to be a Waldorf proponent to appreciate his common sense view:

> Technology, he says, has its time and place: "If I worked at Miramax and made good, artsy, rated R movies, I wouldn't want my kids to see them until they were 17.

Tech aficionados who pretend InfoTech is the only way to make learning fun have a lot to prove. There are many skilled teachers who disagree, and who creatively engage their students, albeit in an ever-challenging and tech-laden environment. For young kids, participative and tactile pedagogies like the Waldorf method offer just what they need: three-dimensional learning in the real world, with the materials and stories that go into keeping people fed, clothed and happy. In contrast, digital enthusiasts like Don Tapscott praise the young tech-savvy students who he says benefit from such democratic digital culture traits as openness, cooperation and sharing.

Tapscott wrote *Growing Up Digital*, a much lauded book, in the late 1990s, and he recently published a sequel, *Grown Up Digital*.

> I came to the conclusion that the defining characteristic of an entire generation was that they were the first to be "growing up digital"... I named them the Net Generation...They outnumbered the boomer adults, I noted, and they were different from any other generation because they were the first to grow up surrounded by digital media. "Today's kids are so bathed in bits that they think it's all part of the natural landscape."[27]

How troubling and provocative is the premise of that last sentence. It assumes that all kids are equally tech savvy and equally engaged online—and that all families and communities are equally able to provide such a tech environment, and that this is something automatically to cheer about.

More curious still is Tapscott's assertion that in embracing digital media "the Net Generation will develop and superimpose its culture on the rest of society." They are, he says, "a force for social transformation." As if this is entirely exciting and positive. To Tapscott's credit, *Grown Up Digital* acknowledges at some length the long line of Internet critics. Although he says, "We should look at their criticisms closely," he also concludes—based on extensive research—that "the Net Generation *has* arrived. And while there are many concerns, overall the kids are more than alright."[28]

As a baby boomer I'm quite surprised by Tapscott's comparison of Net Geners and boomers:

> Eight characteristics, or norms, describe the typical Net Gener and differentiate them from their boomer parents. They prize freedom and freedom of choice. They want to customize things, make them their own. They're natural collaborators, who enjoy a conversation, not a lecture. They'll scrutinize you and your organization. They insist on integrity. They want to have fun, even at work and at school. Speed is normal. Innovation is part of life.[29]

Such sweeping generalizations are unfair to my generation, and they are unfounded. What boomer didn't value freedom and choice? Who says Net Geners excel in conversation? Why elevate fun in school and workplace as the top consideration? Why equate speed with good and normal? Why pretend innovation has just begun? This starkly optimistic image of today's young trashes the spirit of the 60s era that Fritjof Capra captured well in his 2002 essay, "Where Have All the Flowers Gone?"

> For those of us who identify with the cultural and political movements of the sixties, that period represents not so much a decade as a state of consciousness, characterized by "transpersonal" expansion, the questioning of authority, a sense of empowerment, and the experience of sensuous beauty and community. This state of consciousness reached well into the seventies.[30]

Capra touches on the expansion of consciousness, questioning of authority and new sense of community as part of what marked this turbulent and creative period, perhaps best described by Ted Roszak's term *counterculture*. Capra goes on to say:

> ...the most important and enduring legacy of that era has been the creation and subsequent flourishing of a global alternative culture that shares a set of core values. Although many of these values—e.g. environmentalism, feminism, gay rights, global justice—were shaped by cultural movements in the seventies, eighties, and nineties, their essential core was first expressed by the sixties' counterculture. In addition, many of today's senior progressive political activists, writers, and community leaders trace the roots of their original inspiration back to the sixties.[31]

Mark Bauerlein sees today's Net Geners very differently than

Tapscott. In his book *The Dumbest Generation: How the Digital Age Stupefies Young Americans and Jeopardizes Our Nation*, Bauerlein, an English professor at Emory University, views the digital revolution with skepticism bordering on scorn as it pertains to the education of the current "dumbest" generation.

> The Dumbest Generation cares little for history books, civic principles, foreign affairs, comparative religions, and serious media and art, and it knows less. Careening through their formative years, they don't catch the knowledge bug, and *tradition* might as well be a foreign word. Other things monopolize their attention—the allure of screens, peer absorption, career goals...
>
> Fewer books are checked out of public libraries and more videos. More kids go to the mall and fewer to the museum. Lunchroom conversations never drift into ideology, but Web photos pass nonstop from handheld to handheld. If parents and teachers and reporters don't see it now, they're blind.[32]

At the University of Toronto, Kristin Cavoukian, a teaching assistant (TA) and PhD candidate in political science (and my niece), is more than concerned about her students' lack of language skills:

> I've been a T.A. for six years, and I can say that first and second year students have zero command of English. It's getting worse every year! They can't string a sentence together, they make punctuation errors and use words they don't know. The worst of it is, they don't have any understanding of why they ought to care, to care about communicating. Despite all the digital tools they have online (spellcheck, online dictionary, thesaurus), they don't use them! When I'm marking their papers it's easy to see that these students can't (or won't) communicate their points effectively. All the tools are of no use to you, if you don't see the value in using them.[33]

Cavoukian also bemoans the lack of critical thinking in her students. "It's both that they don't *have* the skills, *and* that they can't even appreciate why they should have them," she says. "They're always looking for a shortcut, instead of really learning; they look for instant gratification."

Another problem that keeps coming up, she says, is that "students *assume* the Internet has changed everything for the better. But that's something to be demonstrated, not assumed." She tells me that TAs commiserate on the lack of motivation in their students. "It's a widespread problem."

Facebook Blowback

THE 2012 BOOK *Talking Back to Facebook* by James Steyer (foreword by Chelsea Clinton) is very clear in its portrayal of SM's huge impact on kids and families, and about what parents can and must do in response. Yet the book is more than that. It may also herald a kind of fed-up-with-Facebook feeling, Nicholas Carr's "incipient counter-revolution."[34] The book's author, Jim Steyer of Common Sense Media, explains the book's title:

> I decided to call this book *Talking Back To Facebook* for two reasons: First, Facebook, to me, is the most potent symbol of the digital revolution and the way it's impacting kids and teens. Second, many of the parents and teachers I encountered while researching this book told me how helpless they feel dealing with Facebook and the onslaught of 24/7 digital reality that it represents. They feel isolated in their concerns about how social networks are affecting their kids' way of relating to themselves and others, and they feel overwhelmed and powerless to do anything about it.[35]

Steyer is a highly respected expert in the United States on issues related to children, media and education. An award-winning Stanford professor, he has an impressive and diverse background of advocacy that has led to appearances on notable TV shows including *Oprah, The Today Show, Larry King Live* and *CNN National News.* He is very knowledgeable on the SM dilemma for kids.

> For the past five years, I've been witnessing how social networks, especially Facebook, have transformed the lives of my students at Stanford University, where I teach classes on civil rights, civil liberties, and children's issues. The technology has literally changed the way people relate to each other, get together, and present their image to the world. Interestingly, when I polled my class recently, more than half of my students said they wished Facebook didn't exist. Several of them said they didn't like the way it drained so much of their time and affected their interactions with friends and peers. Many told me that Facebook can diminish the quality and depth of personal relationships and weaken their basic communications skills. But, of course, they *had* to be on it, they said, because everyone else was...
>
> It's distressing to see your kids try to focus on homework when they're being pinged every few minutes by incoming texts, Facebook notifications, and instant messages. Even at a top-flight university like Stanford, I see the impact of this constant distraction in the classroom. During class, many of my students used to routinely check their e-mails and Facebook pages—until I banned the use of laptops during my lectures. Many of today's students are less able to concentrate, write well, think coherently, and synthesize information than they were just a few years ago. And every year they seem to have shallower and shorter attention spans, as well as diminished memory capacity.[36]

In a Common Sense Media video clip, Steyer sums it up this way:

> What we need to do is limit the perils and the problems and maximize the extraordinary opportunities this digital media world presents. That's why I wrote this book, and that's why everybody needs to engage this dialogue. It is really at the centre of what the next generation of young people will look like, and how our society will be shaped for many many decades to come.[37]

That's right, we must "limit the perils and the problems and maximize the extraordinary opportunities." Now ask yourself this: Is it possible to optimize the Lightweb *without* SM reform? Can we maximize digital opportunities *without* constraining the Darkweb? If your answer is No, then you may agree with the central theme of this book.

By acting now to reform SM, we might, in good conscience, be able to enjoy the best of the Lightweb.

Twitter-Free Weekend

ONE FRIDAY NIGHT—January 25, 2013, two years after my SM debut—I tweeted that I'd be taking a Twitter holiday for the weekend. That next morning (Saturday) had a decidedly different quality. Not reaching for Twitter, my habitual morning reflex, had benefits. I allowed myself a Skype call to my niece, who was pregnant, to see how she was doing; after all, that's just like a phone call, I said to myself.

Even in the first hours of this modest SM fast I noticed a difference. I felt subtly more present, "in the room." If I wanted news I could tune in to radio or TV, or surf the Net. My mind was now held back from a two-year habit of tweeting this or that, waiting for RTs (re-tweets) or replies, and appraising new tweeps I might follow. I noticed more clearly my frequent impulse to reach for the Twitter icon on my laptop or smartphone, the Twitter twitch, a Pavlovian move to get a shiny tech treat.

I found myself missing the ever-present distraction I often gave in to, whether to relieve the tension of the moment (I'd say to myself), to let off steam or to take refuge momentarily in other people's challenges—to distract from my own in a given moment. An odd impulse, really, only engaged because it's possible.

I also noticed the desire (or urge) to share with the Twitter community (aka, the Twitterverse) any feelings or thoughts, however trivial. This is the "public living" or "living in social media" now talked and written about—over-sharing, life on display.

When on the second day of my two-day holiday I snuck a quick peek at the "tweethood" and its stream of tweets, familiar names and faces didn't tempt me as before. I found that moment somewhat amusing—to think that one would jump to comment on or reply to someone else's sharing. Yet in the virtual community, you do that. Not a bad thing per se—you can have an exchange, learn something and share useful information. It's just that it's not necessary, and certainly not all the time, not as a way of being. I learned that on an SM fast you can breathe, gain a new perspective and reset your intention to choose. And to avoid compulsion.

I must admit, the Twitter stream (and my public page on Facebook) have been useful. Not only do I get my news first on Twitter; I also enjoy sharing articles of interest with my followers, to give re-tweet support to worthwhile causes and to pass on snippets of advice now and then. From comments I get from many young "tweeps," it seems that I am a mentoring voice on Twitter. And there's been another upside.

When, in early 2012, I considered doing family concerts again (after an absence of 10 years), I floated the idea in a "rumour has it" way on both Twitter and FB to see what the response would be. It was overwhelmingly positive, with fans from all over North America clamouring for a concert near them. It was a factor in confirming my sense that it was time for me to sing in public again.

Twitter's been a lot of fun. As a well-known troubadour, I have found it's useful for me to have a growing SM following: to share thoughts, test ideas and announce concert info or news about a new recording. I like to think I've used Twitter with discernment. Hecklers have been few, and at times they've met with my robust "blocking" instinct. Mostly I've discovered wonderful people, some of whom I've come to know in person and as colleagues.

I've enjoyed coming up with briefly worded ideas and sharing them with, for the most part, an appreciative audience. Writing a tweet can be like the challenge of creating a well-worded headline, with or without a story link or an accompanying photo to post.

It's the compulsive habituation to social media we need to be aware of and resist. "I share therefore I am" is hardly the goal.

Recording Sharing Everything

THERE'S SO MUCH in digital technology we now take for granted that ten years ago we could barely imagine: advances in medicine, data storage and access to online learning tools such as articles, books, podcasts and websites, to name a few. The Internet has become an endless storehouse of information, as well as a source of great distraction. And the smaller portable InfoTech devices play a big part in this.

Back when the video camcorder (with videotape) first came on the market, it was an amazing recording device. It became even more amazing when it could fit into the palm of your hand. When video recording went digital, it went tapeless. And when that feature was offered in a cellphone, people started not only taking photos but also recording at will, simply because they could. It was easy, and fun. So that really changed how we kept track of our personal and family lives.

Birthday parties, special moments, holiday events all get recorded. People don't think twice about posting a video of their kids on SM, or having their own video channel with dozens of personal video clips. I'm amazed at the quality of current video recorders and digital cameras. But I'm taken aback at the amount that people share about the details of their lives.

Pull back for a wider view. We've gone from one-hour photo-finishing (remember that?) to digital photography, cellphone photos and instant sharing; from audio-cassette tapes to CDs to digital music collections in our hands; from camcorders to smartphone videos shared with a touch; from library books on loan to online books and articles searchable in seconds. And yet the benefit to society of such ease and convenience is not clear, when balanced with the costs of such rapid change.

Easy sharing sounds great until you examine its downsides. The easy sharing of music files, for example, is fine if you don't think about the royalty infringements rampant in the digital age. Easy sharing of photos and images is fun, although it can and does lead to over-sharing and poor judgment when done in haste. Information overload is, of course, only part of the not-so-fun endless distraction of being always online.

But perhaps the most disturbing aspect of hyper-sharing is the compulsive need to put so much on display, combined with the temptation to send instant sexual titillations via social networks. Girls send "selfies"—photos of themselves, taken by holding their cellphone at arm's length—to friends for fun and to impress. The pressure to do so, just to keep up with others, is understandable when seen in the context of the growing sexualization of culture.

Pop Goes the Culture

IN LOS ANGELES in the mid-1980s, a single parent casually told me that her 10-year-old son liked to spend Saturday mornings watching MTV. (I cringed; at his age I was watching cartoons.) With a TV in his room, the temptation was great, and his working mother's intervention was next to nil.

During the last few decades, parents have worried about their kids watching MTV videos with violent or sexual content. In the digital age, what can be seen on YouTube makes MTV look tame. And then there are websites like Second Life. Reading Andrew Keen's reference to Second Life,[38] a 3D online society, I visit its website. In the menu, I click on "What Is Second Life" and watch the video "Your World."[39] I am repulsed by this freaky demo with the slogan "Your World, Your Imagination": within seconds, a semi-naked female with a rifle obliterates a ghoulish monster figure...and on it goes, to rhythmic loud music, from one twisted aggressive scenario to another. Above the video screen it says: "Second Life is a 3D world where everyone you see is a real person and every place you visit is built by people just like you."

What? Or, as they say on Twitter, WTF? Below the screen it says: "Enter a world with infinite possibilities and live a life without boundaries, guided only by your imagination." Deception to the max. Parents would hate for their kids to be using such a shallow, distorted excuse for imaginative play. Wouldn't they?

Today, parents who are overworked, stressed and at their wits' end allow the commercial media into their homes. The world of pop commerce relentlessly targets their children 24/7, and parents often feel powerless to defend their turf. What's more, in many households a child's bedroom not only has a TV, but has become InfoTech central, with computerized play stations and shiny tech devices.

Now let me bring your attention to more than the presence of computer technology in kids' rooms. The greater concern is the sexualization of culture.

Consider the role of pop stars in this.

In the 1980s, Madonna and Michael Jackson offered slut stylings and genital groping to a largely adoring and silent media. Feminists like Betty Friedan lauded Madonna and largely ignored the overtly sexual sell of her music videos. Media hardly noticed, let alone commented on, the anger and aggressive sexual gestures in Jackson's videos like "Thriller," "Beat It" and "Billy Jean." Everyone got used to it. It became a new normal, confused with passion. Now 19-year-old pop sensation Justin Bieber, with over 30 million Twitter followers, says he wants to be like Jackson. He definitely seems to be following in Jackson's footsteps, crotch-grabbing repeatedly in his performances.[40]

Such vulgar antics are a worrisome part of the hyper-sexualized pop culture. No media voice called Madonna or Jackson on it, and no one calls Bieber on it now. Why? Since when is lewd public behaviour okay, let alone from a young star with millions of fans?

The problems with hyper-sexualized pop culture are many. It keeps pushing the boundaries and becomes more and more extreme.

The impact on kids is all too real.

In 2004 the *Globe and Mail* and the *Toronto Star* carried stories describing how a growing number of girls in their early teens were performing oral sex on boys to gain friends. Apart from STD health concerns, such age-inappropriate behaviour is an emotional disaster if the girls (and the boys) think that it is cool to trade sexual favours for friendship. Kids that age are too young to navigate the emotional roller coaster of such behaviour. Such actions skew the very notion of friendship at an impressionable age, and peer pressure puts considerable stress on girls who would rather not engage in such promiscuity (although many don't consider it sex if intercourse is not involved). This is sexual coercion, not experimentation. Quite a setback to teens' emotional intelligence.

But should this behaviour surprise us? The sexualization of pop culture is everywhere you look. In Canada, I'm dismayed to see overtly descriptive prime-time TV ads for an erectile dysfunction drug during NHL hockey telecasts on The Sports Network. Recently, the West Edmonton Mall's promotional booklet sported a cover photo of a tween girl with a cowboy hat and a subtly suggestive hostess look. The popular comedy TV show *The Big Bang Theory*, in early prime time, has sexual dialogue with frequent references to "coitus" and "getting laid" that, not long ago, would not have been broadcast.

Twenty years ago, you wouldn't have heard about porn on a CBC morning radio show:

> Good morning. I'm Anna Maria Tremonte and you're listening to *The Current*...Kids on the school bus used to share sandwiches. Now they swap Internet porn. A new documentary looks at how our children are becoming hyper-sexualized.[41]

The proliferation of suggestive images shared on SM prompted programs such as *Sext Up KIDS*, a 2012 CBC-TV documentary on the sexualization of young girls. From the CBC's webpage notes:

> The powder keg that is porn culture has exploded in the lives of North American children. The often-devastating consequences are explored in the new film *Sext up KIDS*.
>
> From tiny tots strutting bikini-clad bodies in beauty pageants to companies marketing itty-bitty thongs and padded bras to 9-year olds, images of ever-younger sexualized girls have become commonplace. Add to that: ever-younger boys with 24-7 access to hard-core internet porn. It saturates their lives — from skate parks to the school bus — by the time they're eighteen, 80 percent of boys are watching porn online. Toss social media into the mix and kids can not only consume

> X-rated images, but can also now produce them. Sexting has become a Grade 7 right of passage.[42]

In the digital age, parenting and education challenges can be overwhelming. My conversations with teachers and parents bear this out. It's as if the integrity of the "village" it takes "to raise a child" gets increasingly undermined.

> Parents and educators struggle to help kids navigate puberty in a world where the line between pop culture and porn culture is increasingly blurred. For every parent who thinks, *"that's not my son or daughter,"* *Sext up KIDS* is your wake up call.[43]

The sexualization of young girls is everywhere you care to look. First there were ill-conceived toddler beauty pageants, and now it's toddler bikinis sold in retail stores. Images of sexuality, both glamorous and promiscuous, reach young girls (and boys) by a variety of pop culture avenues. The cumulative effect of the adult sexual realm pushed into the pre-teen world by direct advertising takes its toll and changes cultural norms.

The Internet brings sexually explicit imagery from the red light district right into your home or even the palm of your hand. Parents who wouldn't think of bringing pornographic materials into their castle now have to be Net savvy to keep it from reaching their young children. Strangely, in Canada and the United States (and elsewhere) there are no legal age restrictions for such websites as there are for cable TV outlets. For parents, this encroachment of explicitly adult domains into kids' lives is a troubling aspect of the Darkweb that now needs monitoring with every online tool at their disposal. It's a pressure-filled situation, and one that rightly worries parents. Family life has not previously had to face *this* kind of chaos.

Remember the "unhealthy culture" that Maslow talked about?

The webpage for a Media Education Foundation documentary *Consuming Kids: The Commercialization of Childhood* tells us:

> With virtually no government oversight or public outcry, the multi-billion-dollar youth marketing industry has used the latest advances in psychology, anthropology, and neuroscience to transform American children into one of the most powerful and profitable consumer demographics in the world.[44]

Susan Linn heads Campaign for a Commercial-Free Childhood, an organization that is (and should be considered) a great friend to families. In her strategic advocacy to keep marketing away from impressionable kids, Linn is a leading children's champion. In *Child Honouring*, an anthology I co-edited, she wrote:

> At this point in time, we can no longer even think about children's media without confronting the unprecedented escalation of child-targeted marketing during the past two decades...The efforts of this gargantuan and ever-expanding industry are linked to myriad childhood ills including the erosion of children's creative play, youth violence, precocious and irresponsible sexuality, childhood obesity, eating disorders, rampant materialism, and family stress.[45]

In the Media Education Foundation documentary *Consuming Kids,* one lively segment sheds more light on the connection between direct marketing to kids and self-image, consumption and the targeted exploitation of the young from birth.

> *Susan Linn:* This generation of children is marketed to as never before. Kids are being marketed to through brand licensing, through product placement, marketing in schools, through stealth marketing, through viral marketing. There's DVDs, there's video games, there's the internet,

> there are iPods, there are cell phones. There are so many more ways of reaching children so that there is a brand in front of a child's face every moment of every day.
>
> *Narrator:* One of the crucial aspects of this trend is that marketers never communicate their adult messages and values to kids simply as kids, but as boys and as girls.
>
> *Diane Levin:* And girls are being taught they need to be pretty, sexy, and what they buy determines their value, and how they look determines their value...
>
> *Juliet Schor:* You see now dolls with highly sexualized outfits and themes marketed to six year olds.
>
> *Narrator:* ... a massive and growing toddler industry that, almost from the womb, now blankets babies in brands.
>
> *Susan Linn:* It's really hard to find baby paraphernalia that's not plastered with media characters...Places where poor or middle class families shop, it's all branded, so the babies start out life with the notion of consumption. And that's not an accident. What they want is cradle to grave brand loyalty. That's what they talk about—share of mind. They talk about owning children for life.[46]

Unconscionable. What else are we to think of the targeting of young children for exploitation, branding them from birth? With personal data mining and digital dossiers forever online, "owning children for life" becomes even more insidious in a vicious circle: brand loyalty, data sold to advertisers who then market to kids for even tighter loyalty. That's why loss of online privacy is one cumulative Darkweb downer.

Privacy Anyone?

SOCIAL MEDIA SELLS our life data to advertisers. That's how we can have SM seemingly "for free." But as mentioned in Part 1, in the op-ed I co-authored with Sandy Garossino, the data-mining aspect of FB and other SM surprised users. Sure surprised me.

At the outset, SM users were not offered a choice between: 1. Free SM with data mining of your life and habits (with advertising), or 2. A low monthly service fee, no data mining, no ads. Had such a choice been offered, I'd have taken option 2 and encouraged everyone else to do the same. This would have certainly protected our privacy and given parents and their kids a degree of security in the wild cyber woods.

Dr Ann Cavoukian, whose "Privacy by Design" concept was described in Part 1, has a clear position on Internet privacy:

> Calls for the imminent death of privacy are fatally flawed. The massive growth of online social networks has led some to believe that there can be no privacy in the future: the more people connect, the less privacy we can have, right? Wrong! This type of classic zero-sum thinking is inherently flawed and should be exposed for the folly it represents. Not only can we have both social contact AND privacy, we must have both.[47]

Individual privacy is a fundamental democratic right.

On that subject we've yet to hear a cogent coherent statement from Facebook's founder, who recently said that privacy has evolved into sharing as a new social norm.[48] A strange comment, given the fundamental role that privacy plays in our lives. Even online, private passwords grant us entry to various sites for all manner of purposes, from banking to gaming to posting comments on news articles to Facebook. Anyone see a problem here?

You can share your holiday photos not just with your FB friends but (whether you want to or not) with advertisers who pay FB to know your life's intimate details, from your favourite beaches and restaurants right down to your bikini styles or contraception choices.[49] Some advertisers are now using photos of Facebook users (even photos of kids) to promote their products: "whenever a user clicks the 'Like' button, Facebook may use that interaction to create an advertisement [which is, ironically, called a "sponsored story"] that is then broadcast to that user's 'Friends' on Facebook—effectively turning every user into a potential spokesperson on behalf of one of Facebook's advertisers. Minors are not exempt from the program, even though several state laws prohibit the use of a minor's likeness without parental consent."[50] Most people either aren't aware that they can be exploited in this way or they don't care. Kids? Even less so.

Imagine, for a moment, if everybody lived online *compulsively* (as many do): constantly hyper-sharing their life experience—*always typing about, recording and sharing life as it happens.*

How can it be good for anyone that their experience of a given moment feels not enough, not "as good" if not shared? I'm not talking about habit here, but compulsion. The seeds of narcissism may take root in the feeling that everything we do is worthy of public interest. That hyper-sharing is the SM virtuality that Mark Zuckerberg and company have invented and now promote full throttle.

NOT SO FAST.

It's one thing for me to remember the real world before SM, yet something totally different for young SM users who cannot know what an immediate (unmediated) and private life feels like. Mark Z may be stealing a way of life. What are we to do about that? Well, for one thing, I can write a letter. Don't have to hit "send."

Dear Mark,

In 1967, when I was 19, the film *The Graduate* was all the rage. The movie's Wikipedia entry has this to say:

> The theme of an innocent and confused youth who is exploited, misdirected, seduced (literally and figuratively) and betrayed by

> a corrupt, decadent, and discredited older generation (that finds its stability in "plastics") was well understood by film audiences and captured the spirit of the times. One of the film's posters proclaimed the difficult coming-of-age for the recent, aimless college graduate.

It was a young Dustin Hoffman—looking a lot like me then—and his film affair with Mrs Robinson that gave rise to the Simon & Garfunkel song of the same name. (It was originally about first lady Mrs Roosevelt; that would explain the "going to the candidates debate" lyric). Both lively and haunting, the recorded version was a big hit. Interestingly, its lyrics and their context in this film have some relevance to our SM moment today.

Its melodic chorus motif includes, "Now here's to you, Mrs Robinson, heaven holds a place for those who pray, hey hey hey...," and the first verse lyrics, "We'd like to know a little bit about you for our files," might eerily evoke today's online data mining and SM postings that create a perpetual file (dossier) of our personal lives.

Mark, you've said that privacy has evolved into the new social norm, sharing. You pretend privacy is no longer needed. It's hard to know what makes you think or say such a silly thing. If it's a self-serving selling tool of a monetizing corporatist, recruiting more millions of users into giving up their privacy, it's terrible. It's also hypocritical. Next time you're out at a restaurant, just try announcing your location to all on FB.

Your SM notions are not a game.

Luring younger and younger kids into using FB without any indication it would be good for them is a brazen attempt to increase FB's profitability. Is this not using the young for your corporate ends? Is this not violating childhood innocence for advertising profits? Is FB turning into a platform for colonizing the child psyche and spirit?

First, do no harm: that's the moral imperative.

Mark, consider the SM intrusion on child development. If kids are *addicted* to the shiny tech machines that are supposed to improve their lives, are they not enslaved? Are shiny tech devices and SM a new form of voluntary slavery?

There's still time. We can change this.

Lightweb Darkweb

AS NOTED EARLIER, by the term Lightweb I'm referring to all the positive attributes of a digitally connected world. Even as we know what these are, we can still be astonished at the benefits of computing power and InfoTech's ability to bring the knowledge world to our fingertips. Darkweb is my term for the previously mentioned negative aspects of the Internet, including the issues of safety, privacy, addiction and more.

On the upside, we hear from some parents of autistic kids that iPads and their visually engaging apps are a boon for expressively challenged kids. The blind and visually impaired can now enjoy print-to-speech reading machines. Speech-recognition software gives those who can't work a keyboard the ability to write with a degree of independence.

The downside, however, might surprise us further: we may yet learn of some shiny tech health issues that make us think twice, make some of us turn away or shock us into some balance. It may be a specific issue or concern. Or it may be a worst case scenario—something systemically unsavoury for our species, and for Nature. (One such example might be the growing recognition of WiFi radiation as a health hazard, which I touched on in Part 1.)

Digital living at the current global level of saturation is still quite new. We don't know how virtuality will affect some aspects of human experience. What does Net dependence do, for example, to our spiritual lives? How do we measure a subtle (yet real) distancing from Nature, and a diminished interest in, or ability to engage in, meditation practice?

And the kids...What is lost in the rush to what we think they're gaining with shiny tech? Does InfoTech become what's most important in their lives? And what are adults for? What are teachers for? What's the value of a real conversation?

Today's kids won't remember a time without digital devices. Can we help them understand how the world was before SM—and if we could, would they care? Can we evoke that world without romanticizing the past?

Seeing Lanier

IF THE INTERNET and InfoTech have become the background of our thoughts, something fundamentally human may be shifting. Our relationship to Nature, our footing on Earth. Our essential experience of human reality.

InfoTech pioneers, brilliant engineers and visionaries, have had diverse motivations in leading this digital revolution. Originally, InfoTech wasn't all about money, though money is very much at the centre of it now. Many were thrilled at the democratic possibilities of an electronically connected world; some were dazzled by the chance to alter reality. By a chance to play God.

In 1995 I saw Jaron Lanier (the so-called father of virtual reality) at a Social Venture Network conference where he and high-tech guru Mitch Kapor shared an evening presentation. Their praises of the Internet made me uneasy; they spoke of its growth as inevitable and unstoppable. Inwardly I recoiled, resisted. (If you weren't online, I wondered, were you expendable, invisible?) Kapor, regarded by many as the Thomas Jefferson of the Internet for his defence of Net freedom, spoke of his Lotus operating system and the coming laptop wave. Lanier was something entirely other. Introduced by spiritual teacher Ram Dass in glowing superlatives, Lanier shared with the audience his passion for what he called virtual reality technology (VR), which he described as where the dream is found. He went on:

> So with VR, I'm not going to go through explaining all the details of it—but I'll show a video of it at the end of our talk for those of you who have never seen it—but it's a technology where you wear computerized clothing over your sense organs and it simulates the experience of being in an alternate world entirely. It doesn't do it very well but it does it well enough that you can buy into it, and most importantly, you can buy into it with other people: you can have an alternate universe that's created by the computer that you share with others. It's big news philosophically, it's the first new objective place since the physical world. And it has a remarkable quality when compared with that old objective place, the physical world.[51]

He was given to making grand statements, so you had to just stay with him and hope for a place to land.

> The source of the magic is the notion that this technology can bridge the interpersonal gap in a fundamentally new way and give flight to the imagination. And the notion of post-symbolic communication, which is that if a generation of kids grew up not only being able to do this but being able to invent things within the world very fluently and very quickly, they would be able to communicate in a new way in addition to symbols, by directly making up stuff instead of referring to stuff indirectly through symbols. Do you follow that? That's a very big deal, that's a really big deal.

Then, in a disjointed way, Lanier alluded to children and their apparent affinity with computer technology.

> This technology is very much the province of young children. Young children get it instinctively; they have a fluency that I certainly don't have, and I'm pretty good at this stuff. They are part of a new culture that's arising which I find wonderful. I find this to be really a great generation gap, because when we look at our children, like children under 10 now have this capacity, I'm sure you've all seen it, and this generation gap is not like a generation gap of increased delinquency or something. It's a generation gap caused by increased ability. We can see it and we can celebrate it, and I just find it so wonderful.

I did not share his enthusiasm. He even claimed that a laptop would produce images of a sunset so beautiful that kids who saw them would want to run outside to see the real thing. I then had to endure a video about VR that had the look and feel of disembodied non-human weirdness.

When the Q & A finally came, up shot my arm. I said I'd worked with little kids for 20 years and strongly objected to the notion that they needed a computer representation of a sunset to enjoy the real thing. Jaron responded with a dismissive "Oh, that's nice." I was dumbfounded. At the close of the session, out of concern for both of us, friends brought Jaron and me together for a private conversation. It didn't help. His eyes darted all over the place.

In the years since that conference, it seems that Lanier's views have changed considerably. On the death of computer pioneer and apologist Joseph Weizenbaum, he wrote a tender eulogy:

> History will remember Weizenbaum as the clearest thinker about the philosophy of computation. A metaphysical confrontation dominated

> his interactions with the non-human-centered mainstream. There were endless arguments about whether people were special in ways that cybernetic artifacts could never be. The mainstream preferred to sprinkle the magic dust of specialness on the "instruments," as Weizenbaum put it, instead of people.
>
> But there was a less metaphysical side of Weizenbaum's thinking that is urgently applicable to the most pressing problems we all face right now. He warned that if you believe in computers too much, you lose touch with reality. That's the real danger of the magic dust so liberally sprinkled by the mainstream. We pass this fallacy from the lab out into the world. This is what apparently happened to Wall Street traders in fomenting a series of massive financial failures. Computers can be used rather too easily to improve the efficiency with which we lie to ourselves. This is the side of Weizenbaum that I wish was better known.[52]

Today, Lanier is a critic of the Net's "hive mind." His book *You Are Not a Gadget* is driving people to write blogs titled "Why Does Jaron Lanier Hate the Web So Much?"[53] They should heed his current caution:

> We wouldn't let a student become a professional medical researcher without learning about double blind experiments, control groups, placebos, the replication of results, and so on. Why is computer science given a unique pass that allows us to be soft on ourselves? Every computer science student should be trained in Weizenbaumian skepticism, and should try to pass that precious discipline along to the users of our inventions.[54]

Being Human

BILL MCKIBBEN'S brilliant book *Enough: Staying Human in an Engineered Age* examines a wide range of emerging technologies (cloning, genetic engineering, robotics, nanotech) that "call into question, often quite explicitly, our understanding of what it is to be a human being." McKibben asks: "Must we forever grow in reach and power? Or can we, should we, ever say, 'Enough'?"[55]

McKibben is a leader in the campaign to address the global climate threat. His vision of living sustainably on our one and only planet, within the limits of its tolerance for supporting life, is quite different than that of the digerati, who would have us augment our lives in every high-tech way possible.

A leading inventor, cyber-utopian futurist Ray Kurzweil recently joined Google as director of engineering. In a Google Talks presentation, he lays out his futuristic vision of computing as brain expanding and search engines as our 24/7 assistants.[56] Kurzweil is long on the human brain's pattern-recognition architecture—30 billion neurons arranged per 100 into 300 million modules that connect hierarchically—but short on the feeling state of being human. Intelligence is presented as computing power. The role of the heart is missing.

Kurzweil and other digi-enthusiasts are excited by the endless promise of InfoTech. They give many convincing examples of how it improves people's lives. As for me, I'm also glad for many of the technological wonders we now take for granted (including painless dental care and worldwide air travel). And I marvel at the laptop and smartphone at my side and how they operate. However, I'm not blind to social and environmental costs incurred in the making and use of these conveniences. I care about the social injustice of forced labour in factories overseas where teens day after mind-numbing day assemble these shiny gadgets. And increasingly, I worry about the health risks to a population hooked on wireless tech, with its microwave radiation pollution all around and on our electromagnetic bodies.

Ray Kurzweil speaks of a post-biological future and predicts that exponentially growing computational power will allow human intelligence to merge with artificial intelligence in various forms of enhanced living. In his book *The Age of Spiritual Machines*, one of his timeline predictions for the year 2019 is: "Computers are now largely invisible and are embedded everywhere—in walls, tables, chairs, desks, clothing, jewelry, and bodies."[57] This does not give me a warm feeling.

SM reform is one thing; "re-forming humans" another thing entirely. Tinkering with the very nature of what it is to be human is not for the faint of heart.

Astonishingly, Kurzweil seems to ignore such biological basics as our central nervous system, womb and birth experience, lactation and so on. Children do not merit an entry in this book's index, nor in the index of his latest, *How to Create a Mind*. About that work, I was glad to read Colin McGinn's sound critique in the *New York Review of Books*, where McGinn described it as "moderately informative, but wildly overstated."[58]

Google Glass, a Kurzweil invention, was launched to mixed reviews recently. These "smart glass" specs have a camera and screen on the right side, and you can search the web by speaking your request or command. At over a thousand dollars, GG is a costly, fragile and completely unnecessary InfoTech device—to my mind, the dumbest yet. If this is any indication of the future of "wearable" computing, I imagine (and hope) it's in for a bumpy ride.

I'm not that concerned with which of Kurzweil's predictions will be right or wrong. My worry is for the developing intelligence of young children, older kids, adolescents and a society bent on distractedly postponing its maturation.

In Kurzweil's brainy calculations, where is the role of the heart? Does he really equate human intelligence with mere computational capacity? That's the impression one gets. But how can that be? This is a highly intelligent man and, I hear, a wonderful person. Can there be a basic human flaw in his cyber dreams?

Can Descartes' fundamental error—seeing the human as a machine —now be driving a Kurzweil-led Google at warp speed?

Re-Forming Life

All the king's horses and all the king's men
couldn't put Humpty together again.
~ Nursery rhyme

If you don't know how to fix it, stop breaking it.
~ Severn Cullis-Suzuki, 12, Rio Earth Summit (1992)

DO CYBER UTOPIANS suffer from a basic tech-induced myopia? Or is it digital hubris? Or, to come at the question another way, are they in a state of existential despair, one that's too painful to bear? Do they put all their money on tech fixes instead of organic healing processes? Are they eco-imaginally challenged? Why are they not as enamoured, say, with eco-literacy and biomimicry, the appreciation of Nature's unfathomable intricacy and design wonders? Where is *that* wonderment? Is it too messy?

Speaking of messy, that concept is foreign to a sleek five-minute video made by Corning, a name we know as a maker of glass cookware. *A Day Made of Glass* starts at "7:00 am In The Near Future" with a couple waking up and, with their kids, going about their day—one in which glass plays a very big part.[59] Photovoltaic glass, LCD television glass (touch screen), architectural display glass (touch screen in bathroom), architectural surface glass (kitchen counter touch screen), appliance veneer glass (touch screen fridge door), handheld display glass (smartphone), automotive display glass (in car) are only some of what's featured in this futuristic vision of apparently antiseptic living. By the time you get to the flexible display glass, you might wonder how much this stuff costs, how fragile it is and how un-cool you'd be to take a pass on so much glass. "Perfect for augmenting reality," the narrator says in the follow-up video.[60]

Here's another glimpse of where InfoTech is heading.

I was stunned by one slide in particular in an 88-slide report by Mary Meeker and Liang Wu of venture capital firm KPCB. "2012 Internet Trends" was full of stats and then-vs-now comparisons of past practices and new models in a number of sectors.[61] "Re-imagination of nearly everything" is what they're boasting. And they've got some data on that.

In this informative show, you learn that in 2002, "after 125 years, landlines were surpassed by mobiles." And that after 244 years of being the symbol of important accumulated knowledge, *Encyclopedia Britannica* went out of print in 2012. Some then–now contrasts are quite striking: a red UK phone booth vs a cellphone held by an Asian user. Some, not so: a woman doing an oil painting vs a tablet drawing program. This is a digital native's heaven. And, perhaps, a digital immigrant's purgatory (or hell).

Slide after slide there's an unspoken yet unmistakable impression conveyed: everything that went before was so...cumbersome—"ancient," as the kids now say. Defunct.

In the slide "Re-Imagination of Learning," the "Then..." side has a classroom image out of the 1960s: a girl with her arm raised and a teacher at the green board (with some arithmetic tables), both with their backs to the camera. The "Now..." side shows two images: one, a baby sitting up and looking at an iPad; the second, a 3-year-old standing and about to touch a smart screen of some kind—no adults to be seen.

This is not re-imagining. It's madness.

Virtuality

THERE'S NO QUESTION that SM has hugely impacted family life and altered social rhythms. For all its benefits, it's also true that, for a number of reasons, it's a nuisance.

Parents complain that their teens want to take their cellphones to bed with them, and this causes arguments. Many parents have a "no cellphone at night" rule, and their kids must leave the devices on the kitchen table. Others say they lock up the cellphones at night. You can imagine the hassles that ensue. Such is the power of virtual connection, distraction, dependency, addiction (take your choice).

Moms and dads: ten years ago parenting had no such issue. Life was full of real everyday challenges. Now, family space has been hijacked by the very devices that are supposed to enhance our lives. They've taken over the family dynamic. Before shiny tech, the main parenting challenges were sex, religion, discipline and dating, in terms of what, when and how you engaged these topics. Now, on top of all that, you have the added burden of regulating the real and virtual divide on a daily basis. Having "the talk" with kids meant sex education; now it needs to include the Internet and SM too.

Ongoing vigilance isn't fun. Yet vigilance is precisely what cyber safety experts urge of parents in order to keep their SM kids safe. But that's not a realistic option, for parents *or* for kids. What home wants to be a den of suspicion and constant surveillance?

Mediated living (overconnection, virtuality) removes you one more step from the real world. The background of your thoughts becomes SM and its hyper-pulse: it changes your mind, alters your rhythms, makes a second self, as Sherry Turkle put it—the always available you. Your private space shrinks, without your awareness. Your interiors, once the place of solitude and wonder, now crowded or hard to access, become almost foreign, no longer a place of refuge. You seek comfort outside. If you're an adult, you may understand this process. Not so for kids. How can they know what's happening to them? What would they compare it to?

In the wider world, the much-touted democratization of knowledge and instant communication hasn't helped strengthen democracy, as Evgeny Morozov makes clear in *The Net Delusion*.[62] Reading Douglas Rushkoff's book *Life Inc.*, we're reminded that the corporation, a virtual entity, dominates society, and in the United States was given "person" status by the Supreme Court.[63] Interesting, then, and not too surprising, that SM virtuality proliferates. America's highest court blurs the real and the virtual; the people follow suit.

There's no app for wisdom. If you're not grounded in the real world, if you can't face the complexity of being fully human, how can you possibly thrive in navigating virtuality—or even tell the difference?

The New Electricity

IT'S LIKE SOCIETY has a new electric switch. With computers and personal tech devices we flip that switch. It's a current with a lot of signal: too hot to handle for young users, the unintended players.

With constant texting, browsing, posting, sharing, does the brave new tech world's information tsunami distract us to triviality? Are we "amusing ourselves to death," as Neil Postman suggested in 1985? In that book's foreword he wrote:

> Orwell warns that we will be overcome by an externally imposed oppression. But in Huxley's vision, no Big Brother is required to deprive people of their autonomy, maturity and history. As he saw it, people will come to love their oppression, to adore the technologies that undo their capacities to think...
>
> Orwell feared those who would deprive us of information. Huxley feared those who would give us so much that we would be reduced to passivity and egoism. Orwell feared that the truth would be concealed from us. Huxley feared the truth would be drowned in a sea of irrelevance. Orwell feared we would become a captive culture. Huxley feared we would become a trivial culture.[64]

Postman cites Huxley's comment on our "almost infinite appetite for distraction" as a key driver in "amusing ourselves to death." He writes, "Orwell feared that what we hate will ruin us. Huxley feared that what we love will ruin us."[65] It would appear that both were right. Human societies have elements of misplaced fear and misguided love. And the cumulative effect is a kind of paralysis regarding the survival needs of our species. A paralysis brought on largely by distraction. Or fear. (Or both.) A state that drives us into compulsive consumption.

To overcome that fear and distraction, we must tap into our intelligence and empathy, the moral sensitivity Darwin described.

Love and Anxiety

TWO DRIVERS OF formative human development are love and anxiety. Love is the primary nutrient in the ecology of the child. And the quality of that love is important to the reduction of anxiety. "Love," says Chilean biologist Humberto Maturana, "is the only emotion that expands intelligence."[66] "Anxiety," child development author Joseph C. Pearce observes, "is the great crippler of intelligence."[67] *Love is the only emotion that expands intelligence. Anxiety is the great crippler of intelligence.*

From this it follows that nations wanting to increase the intelligence of their citizens should do all they can to ensure that newborns begin life nested in respectful love and positive attachment, growing with minimal anxiety in the critically important first years.[68] This is because the emotional tone of being is set in highly formative early impressions and experiences. How infants are regarded and treated by their caregivers and their community becomes what they absorb as possibility or constraint in forming a sense of self in the world.

For expanding intelligence, an efficiency model of birthing and childrearing does not work. That simply produces a culture of anxiety, easily prone to addictions, consumerism and narcissism: what we see way too much of. What's needed is the grounded confidence of children steeped in emotional intelligence,[69] growing up unhurried by parents who understand the benefits of such faith in life.

As Dan Goleman pointed out in his groundbreaking book *Emotional Intelligence*, IQ may get you hired, but EQ will get you a promotion.[70] For the young child, EQ is formed in active play, in exploring the arts, in books and songs, in learning the art of cooperation. For all of us, it's about being emotionally aware and expressive, respecting diversity and behaving responsibly. It's about living with empathy and compassion.

The theory of multiple intelligences that Howard Gardner introduced is important to mention here.[71] Each of us has a diversity of abilities, different intelligences for moving through life. In the digital age, staying grounded in the real world is the necessary compass for navigating the online world. Perhaps, as well, an altogether new intelligence is required—call it Internet Intelligence: the ability to navigate the virtual world.

In our communities and in the population at large, we want to optimize the chances for love to grow and for anxiety to subside. Life has enough real-world drama without adding unnecessary suffering due to ignorance. We know too much to overlook the indispensable benefits of grounding our children in respectful love from birth.

The interconnected web of life needs care and protection, and SM reform now can help optimize our Lightweb experience and send all the right signals to our young. Remember the caution from Jim Steyer and Chelsea Clinton at the end of Part 1: if "managed well," if we act to subdue the Darkweb, the Net might live up to its promise of great opportunity.

We have a chance for a digital mid-course correction so that we can truly connect in our highest aspirations: to create caring, sustaining and peace-making societies.

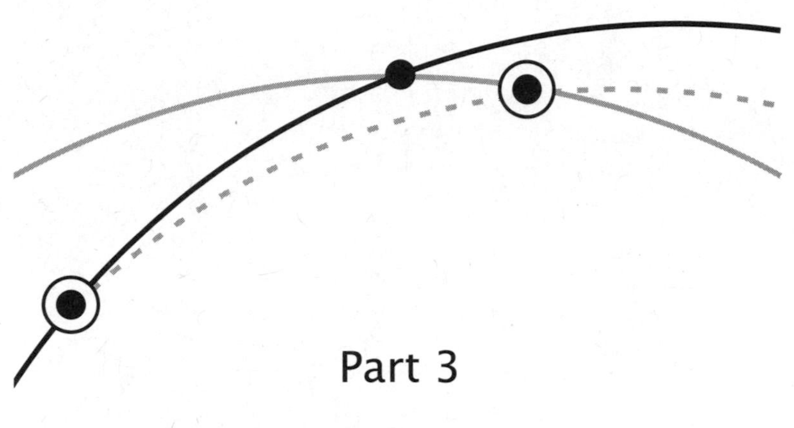

Part 3

SUSTAINABILITY

#lightwebdarkweb

If not for reverence, if not for wonder, if not for love,
why have we come here?
~ from the song "Tomorrow's Children," Raffi

SAFETY AND INTELLIGENCE are two very good reasons for immediate reform of social media. Another good reason for reform is sustainability. As it pertains to the digital age, "sustainability" refers to the ecology of InfoTech: its manufacture, marketing and life cycle. This is what brings SM to our fingertips.

Sustainability?

It's not just about conserving the life-giving qualities of air, water and soil. It's about a way of living ethically, a code of conduct for our relations with the Earth, with each other and with the future. It's a promise of love for generations: for our children and grandchildren, and for generations to come. And it's one of nine principles that arise from A Covenant for Honouring Children, a foundation of the Child Honouring philosophy.[1]

Sustainability is not for cowards—it's the brave new world of responsibility. For Earth and child. For family. For futures worth living.

Sustainability is about *authentic* corporate social responsibility (CSR).

It's also about the personal responsibility of consciously made decisions on what we'll buy and why. It's about the eco-awareness of how our purchasing decisions affect others in the human family.

It's about what stories we tell our children, what they are taught in school and what they may dream of becoming when they grow up. All this adds up to the quality of their future lives.

Politicians like to assure us that all is well, even when we know otherwise. In the post-Fukushima age, with the radiation-spewing breakdown of nuclear power, we might wonder if our species is about to realize the true costs of doing business within an economic model in which people and planet don't count.

Rare Earth

SO YOU'RE SITTING in your favourite coffee hangout with your smartphone or tablet and feeling so cool to be searching the web, accessing this or that, checking out your new apps—and then it happens. A friend sends you an online article that hits you between the eyes: "Your Smartphone's Dirty, Radioactive Secret." There goes the day.

Conscience. Stirs up trouble. The article's subtitle says, "The rare earths inside microcomputers make our lives easier. But just how toxic are the guts of your smartphone?"[2] Quite toxic, as it turns out.

Who wants to read this? "The elements that power all our high-tech gadgets come from a very dirty industry in which rich nations extract the good stuff from the earth—and leave poor countries to clean up the mess." You can't help it. You realize you care.

So you do some digging and you find other online articles. You learn of 17 rare earth elements (REEs) with exotic names, all ending in "ium," that are used "extensively in a wide variety of applications to make technologies lighter, stronger, more efficient, and easier to use."[3]

Mining of these elements (Wikipedia tells you), along with refining and recycling them, can have "serious environmental consequences if not properly managed." Radioactive tailings in waste, toxic acids in refining...by now your latte is losing its allure. But wait, it's not just the InfoTech industry that uses REEs. Electric and hybrid cars also use them. Same with wind turbines. Even LED and compact fluorescent light bulbs. (Oh, and the military too.) OMG.

At this point you remember that, yes, much of the commerce that brings cheaply priced goods to consumers has a big ecological footprint. You order another latte. Double shot.

Why does the global marketplace hide so much about what goes into the goods that come to market and how they are sourced and made?

The insatiable marketing of tech gadgets to an ever-consuming public has a profound downside (read *dark side*) that most of us are simply not aware of.

Reading on in the "Dirty Secret" article takes a force of will. Lynas Corporation in Malaysia, one of the companies involved in REE refinery operations without "a long-term storage solution for the waste," has a website with a "Zero Harm and Sustainable Development" link on its home page, and an "Our goal is Zero Harm" message on the clicked page. Yet the "Dirty Secret" article details that company's distinct lack of transparency in its operations. Something's not quite right.

You've just had another glimpse of the Darkweb.

Inside Apple

LET'S GET PERSONAL.

Would you want your son or daughter working 12-hour shifts for next to nothing, doing mind-numbing, repetitive tasks for weeks and months on end, and living in cramped, multiple-storey lodgings draped with suicide-prevention netting? If not, ask yourself: How do I feel about my infatuation with the digital devices that come from such hard labour and brutal conditions?

Do you like the idea of your computer waste poisoning families in India who dismantle your e-trash? If you don't, what do you think about the obsolescence factor of relentlessly marketed new-and-improved shiny tech devices?

Does it matter to you that the rare earth minerals that go into the manufacture of these devices are extracted in dangerous and polluting conditions?

Bright HDTV ads for shiny tech won't tell you about this dark side. The gadgets look fantastic! Wow, look at those sleek iPads in coloured cases, might as well buy two or three; they're the new Swatch, only much better. Oh how thrilling, this world of tech design—and so shiny.

Fasten your seatbelt. Here's an ABC News exclusive:

> Tens of millions of people around the world have opened one of those sublime white boxes to marvel at the brilliance of the iPad, but no one from the outside has ever seen how these machines are built. Until now.
>
> Hey, everybody, I'm Bill Weir, ABC News *Nightline*. Welcome to Chengdu, China; welcome to Foxconn. As Apple's top supplier, this massive company has earned the worst kind of headlines in recent years. So many of their employees jumped from the roofs of their factories they've put up suicide nets. After word got out, hundreds of thousands of Apple fans called on that company to reform working conditions inside.
>
> After years of intense privacy, Apple invited us to their supply chain. So on a special Tuesday night edition of *Nightline* we will show you how your iPad, your iPhone, your MacBook is made. And we will meet the people who made them.
>
> We'll show you how these folks come on buses, sometimes for days, to travel to the Foxconn gates, desperate for a chance to wipe a screen or solder a chip for ten hours a day, for less than a dollar fifty an hour. I'll interview a top Foxconn executive about those suicides,

> about how things have changed ever since, and we'll hear how Apple polices itself by ordering the largest independent audit this industry has ever seen. It's a fascinating look into a hidden corner of our world.[4]

ABC News tells us that

- there are 141 steps in manufacturing an iPhone;
- many workers in the Foxconn factory are 17, 18 years old;
- many came from the poor villages out in the countryside with the hope of making two dollars an hour;
- the sleek machines that dazzle...are mostly made by hand;
- it takes around five days and 325 sets of hands to assemble an iPad;
- 12-hour shifts are broken up by two hour-long meal breaks;
- after 12 hours...many head home to a nearby dorm room they share with seven other workers;
- suicide nets went up in the spring of 2010 when nine Foxconn workers jumped to their deaths in a span of three months.[5]

In the glare of such media disclosure, Apple has tightened up its management of Foxconn and other sub-contractors and is now partnering with the Fair Labor Association to work towards improved labour practices. Well done, *Nightline*! You helped spur some positive change. But as many watchdog groups continue to point out, Apple and the other major tech brands have a long way to go.[6]

Challenging the Chip

YOU SEARCH FURTHER online and find the video *The Story of Electronics* and the book *Challenging the Chip.*

Annie Leonard, who appears in and narrates *The Story of*

Electronics, is a brilliant communicator whose stick-figure animated videos expose and challenge "the take/make/waste system that's trashing the planet, harming our health, and endangering communities." (Her debut video, *The Story of Stuff*, fast became an Internet hit with millions of views.[7]) The website's description paints a clear picture:

> The Story of Electronics employs the Story of Stuff style to explore the high-tech revolution's collateral damage—25 million tons of e-waste and counting, poisoned workers and a public left holding the bill. Host Annie Leonard takes viewers from the mines and factories where our gadgets begin to the horrific backyard recycling shops in China where many end up. The film concludes with a call for a green "race to the top" where designers compete to make long-lasting, toxic-free products that are fully and easily recyclable.[8]

"A green race to the top" is just what the late Ray Anderson, CEO of Interface, Inc., became devoted to: climbing Mt Sustainability, as he put it.[9] Among the many that he inspired was Annie Leonard.

Leonard travelled the world for ten years to learn first-hand about "the materials economy" of stuff: extraction, production, distribution, consumption and disposal. She has worked on a range of short but informative "Story of..." videos, and her website provides many resources for those who want to learn more about the themes presented in these videos. She gets us thinking about the materials economy as an unsustainable system in crisis.

I needed to find out more about digital tech and sustainability, and luckily I found an amazing source of information in Ted Smith.

Greening the electronics industry has been Smith's work for 30 years. The Silicon Valley resident co-edited the anthology *Challenging the Chip: Labor Rights and Environmental Justice in the Global Electronics Industry*. If you're a newcomer to such ideas as labour rights and environmental justice, just imagine your own family working in toxic conditions the way families of high-tech workers overseas have been and are to this day. Consider the most basic aspects of fairness in how people should be treated—those who slave to produce the consumer goods we enjoy.

> Of the millions of words written over the past several decades about the electronics industry's incredible transformation of our world, far too few have addressed the downsides of this revolution. Many are surprised to learn that environmental degradation and occupational health hazards are as much a part of high-tech manufacturing as miniaturization and other such marvels.[10]

As a relative newcomer to this issue myself, I was appalled to learn that most InfoTech devices are assembled by people in "working conditions as dangerous as those in the early industrial era in Europe and the United States," and that "the health and ecological footprints of the global electronics industry remain largely hidden from most consumers' view."[11]

It takes the shine off shiny tech when you pause to consider that contamination of workers and their surroundings has been a shadow side of the InfoTech boom all along. Add to that the near-sweatshop conditions in which many workers toil in order to feed the great demand for these products, and it certainly taints the InfoTech picture. Smith and the co-editors of this anthology make clear that their aim is not to blame but, rather, to "re-articulate responsibility and provide a vision of what a sustainable electronics industry can look like."[12]

Social media, meet CSR, meet social justice.

Smith says the book "grew out of a global symposium sponsored by the Silicon Valley Toxics Coalition [which he founded] and the International Campaign for Responsible Technology in 2002 where people from 15 countries came together to share experiences and common challenges."[13]

The resulting anthology is a comprehensive documentation of the dark side of the InfoTech revolution, featuring many contributors whose work in pursuit of a responsible electronics vision deserves to be known. One chapter of the book documents the history of high-tech development in Silicon Valley itself, including the sorry saga of how pollution from the emerging chip industry prompted the US Environmental Protection Agency to list 29 toxic sites as federal Superfund sites, with the highest concentration of contamination in theUnited States. Other chapters cover a range of topics as diverse as electronic design, chip manufacture, high-tech pollution, labour conditions, e-waste and recycling, and even "extended producer responsibility legislation"—all providing a close look at the underbelly of the InfoTech industry. Reports from many countries involved in the high-tech industry show that unsustainable computing is a global issue that needs global attention.

If you dream of a sustainable computing industry, as I often do, it is heartening to find someone like Ted Smith, who is passionate about it: "*Challenging the Chip* is about challenging the industry to use its incredible ingenuity to *dazzle the world all over again* [italics mine] with cleaner, greener technologies, products, and components that are free of toxics, easy to recycle, and produced without harm to those manufacturing, assembling, and disassembling them."[14] Smith says that the planned obsolescence of electronic devices, which become outdated very quickly, virtually rules out repairing or upgrading existing ones, and that forces consumers to buy new devices and throw out the old.

> The rapid pace of change is a real double-edged sword because new chemicals are being incorporated before adequate health testing is done, and we are also consuming faster than we can recycle.[15]

Asked if a sustainable electronics industry is viable, his answer is simple and makes sense: "An industry that's been able to put thousands of songs, photos, and videos on a tiny chip has the capacity to pave the way towards a sustainable future."[16]

Challenging the Chip is, among other things, a primer on social and environmental responsibility in the digital age. Imagine if it were high school curriculum material, required reading for every student. And if every student knew the name Annie Leonard and, inspired by her videos, asked two simple questions about stuff: Where does it come from? and Where does it go?—sustainability questions for transforming the materials economy.

Imitating Life's Genius

LET ME TELL you more about Ray Anderson, the sustainability innovator I mentioned earlier. This man had a mid-life epiphany after reading *The Ecology of Commerce*.[17] He totally turned his company around. He directed Interface, his floor-coverings giant (with sales in over a hundred countries), on a path to Mission Zero: no carbon footprint while chalking up impressive numbers on energy saved, CO_2 offsets and increased profitability. In his book *Business Lessons from a Radical Industrialist*, he bemoans "our dangerous faith in a broken industrial model that is yoked to our infatuation of stuff—namely, consumerism."[18]

To those who think sustainability is some hard-to-define idea, I say, "Don't be lazy; read Ray Anderson."

- A sustainable society, into the indefinite future, will accept and honour the fragile finiteness of earth.
- A sustainable society will adopt the truly long view and put humans in their proper relationship with and within nature.

- A sustainable society will build on the ascendancy of women in business, the professions, the government, and education.
- In a sustainable society, technologies will share different general characteristics. They will be renewable, cyclical, solar-driven, waste-free, benign, and focused on resource productivity.

> This is the big challenge. This is humankind's opportunity. This is the better way. That way is sustainability: the survival option.[19]

Speaking of innovation, in her extraordinary TED talks "The Promise of Biomimicry" and "Biomimicry in Action," Janine Benyus offers a new lens for learning from life. Not cheating or distorting life—imitating it. This is *life-changing* in the best sense of that term. It changes *our* lives by giving us new sight, by stirring our imagination.

Benyus describes Nature's laboratory as having 3.8 billion years of field-testing, with 10 to 30 million species comprising, as she puts it, the same number of well-adapted solutions.

> Learning about the natural world is one thing; learning *from* the natural world—that's the switch. That's the profound switch...The important thing for me is that these are solutions [found] in context. And the context is the Earth — the same context that we're trying to solve our problems in.[20]

Biomimicry is "the *conscious* emulation of life's genius...It's taking the design principles, the genius of the natural world, and learning something from it." I absolutely love this; it's innovation with benign design: safe, intelligent, sustainable.

The most important thing, Benyus tells us, is that the biological organisms she highlights in her talk "have figured out a way to do the amazing things they do while taking care of the place that's going to take care of their offspring...That's the biggest design challenge."

There it is: respecting Earth and Child. Respect Mother Earth so your young can prosper. What could be clearer?

Benyus is passionate about biomimicry throughout her talk, but even more so in her closing:

> Those organisms that have not been able to figure out how to enhance or sweeten their places are no longer around to tell us about it...Life creates conditions conducive to life. It builds soil; it cleans air; it cleans water, it mixes the cocktail of gases that you and I need to live...We have to find a way to meet our needs, while making of this place an Eden.[21]

In her 2009 TED talk, with a riveting slide show of Nature's exquisite geometry and art forms, Benyus opens with these memorable words:

> If I could reveal anything that is hidden from us, at least in modern cultures, it would be to reveal something that is forgotten, that we used to know as well as we used to know our own names. And that is, that we live in a competent universe, that we are part of a brilliant planet, and that we are surrounded by genius. Biomimicry is a new discipline that tries to learn from those geniuses and take advice from them, design advice...
>
> Imagine designing Spring. Imagine that orchestration...Imagine the timing, the coordination, all without top-down laws, or policies, or climate change protocols. This happens every year. There is lots of showing off. There is lots of love in the air. There's lots of grand openings. And the organisms, I promise you, have all of their priorities in order.[22]

We are reminded that all the organisms of the natural world are doing things to thrive, much as we need to do. The one stark difference is that they do them in a way that allows them to survive for millennia.

Benyus challenges innovators to lead with this question: "What if, every time I started to invent something, I asked, 'How would Nature solve this?'"

> There's a group of scientists in Cornell who are making what they call a synthetic tree, because they are saying, "There is no pump at the bottom of a tree." Its capillary action and transpiration pulls water up, a drop at a time, pulling it, releasing it from a leaf and pulling it up through the roots. And they're creating—you can think of it as a kind of wallpaper. They're thinking about putting it on the insides of buildings to move water up without pumps...
>
> And we're working with EOL, Encyclopedia of Life, Ed Wilson's TED wish. And he's gathering all biological information on one website. And the scientists who are contributing to EOL are answering a question, "What can we learn from this organism?" And that information will go into AskNature.org. And hopefully, any inventor, anywhere in the world, will be able, in the moment of creation, to type in, "How does nature remove salt from water?" And up will come mangroves and sea turtles and your own kidneys.

Biomimicry, I think to myself, is the discipline of benign design. Studying Nature's library for the countless stories of living and thriving. And imitating, if only for our very survival. For sustaining civilization.

Personal Responsibility

SUSTAINABILITY IS ABOUT the very basis of our relationship with Nature, the foundation of all that's possible. And it's about our relations with each other and with the generations to come. As Paul Hawken's brilliant book *The Ecology of Commerce* made abundantly clear, it's about the restorative dance of purification, detoxification, redesign, rejuvenation. Yet how many of InfoTech's leaders have read that book or taken it to heart?

The rapid rise of the digital revolution and shiny tech displaced the eco-revolution Al Gore wrote about in *Earth in the Balance*,[23] which he apparently traded for "free trade," with its thinned national borders (for corporations), job outsourcing and relentless 24/7 commerce worldwide.

A global gold rush has been on for some time. As I wrote in my autobiography:

> In *The Road Ahead* by Bill Gates, there's a chapter called "Friction-free Capitalism." The grand idea here seems to be that we should all have (via the Net) the ability to buy whatever we want, at any time of day or night, from wherever in the world we can get it the cheapest. But that is simply the polar opposite to ecological thinking, which stresses short supply lines, bioregional sufficiency and full-cost accounting.
>
> It stands to reason, then, that in the global economy's ever widening gap between the haves and have-nots, the drive to "have it all" can only come at an inestimable cost. For the have-nots, for those living off-line, for indigenous cultures—in fact, for anyone not playing the Net game—the game gets tougher and they fall farther behind along the way. And those out to win at all costs turn playing fields toxic and strip the garden bare. As Vancouver ecologist Bill Rees has pointed out, for everyone on Earth to live the North American lifestyle, it would take the resources of three-and-a-half such planets.[24]

Friction-free capitalism? Friction-free for whom? What friction? Labour rights, social justice, national sovereignty, environmental laws, democracy, basic human rights—are we to think of these as friction? And today, are we to view the safety of young SM users as "friction" that slows corporate profits?

As noted earlier, the three reasons for reforming social media go together. If young user *safety* can't be assured, that's a serious defect. If user *intelligence* is compromised, that too is a very high price to pay for virtual connection and info gathering. *If the entire ecology of InfoTech devices harms people and pollutes the Earth, how is the social media infrastructure at all sustainable?*

If only InfoTech leaders would have mid-life (or early life) epiphanies like the one Ray Anderson had while he was head of Interface, the Atlanta-based floor-coverings company. I knew Ray; he was a gentleman. And he was a leader in the sustainability movement in business.

Anderson had a life-altering awakening when he realized that his company was, as he put it, a plunderer of the Earth. He didn't waste a moment. He turned Interface into a champion of sustainability, and he produced the bottom-line numbers to show why every business needs to "climb Mt Sustainability." And he put the case for sustainability in the plainest language I've ever seen: "The economy is a subset of Nature, not vice versa. I've never seen the business case for *un*-sustainability."

What if Bill Gates were to have a similar epiphany, realizing that the future health of his family—and indeed the global human family—depends on the deep greening of InfoTech? What if he were to commit himself to the thorough detoxification of the electronics industry by bringing his influence to bear on leaders in InfoTech and beyond? What if he and other industry leaders were to publicly declare that InfoTech must prioritize the next generation of children the way it currently prioritizes the next generation of chips? What a lasting legacy that would be!

Wanted: epiphanies—in the hearts and minds of all industry leaders. Sustainability is the highest road in the shift to a smart, caring economy.

As members of the privileged minorities in "developed" countries, most of us don't think much about the full cost of a product we buy, beyond its monetary cost. And when shopping, most people usually look for the comparatively lowest-priced item.

Yet in recent years, growing numbers of shoppers have come to care about the way goods are brought to market. "Fair trade" as a concept has caught the imagination of caring consumers who want to minimize the social and environmental footprint of marketed technologies and conveniences. On the Fairtrade.ca website, I found this description:

> Fair Trade (also known as "fair trade" or "fairly traded") refers to the broader concept of fairness and decency in the marketplace...
>
> Fair Trade is a different way of doing business. It's about making principles of fairness and decency mean something in the marketplace.
>
> It seeks to change the terms of trade for the products we buy—to ensure the farmers and artisans behind those products get a better deal. Most often this is understood to mean better prices for producers, but it often means longer-term and more meaningful trading relationships as well.
>
> For consumers and businesses, it's also about information. Fair Trade is a way for all of us to identify products that meet our values so we can make choices that have a positive impact on the world.[25]

In this light, I've sent out tweets saying, "If you're not for *fair* trade, what are you for?"

Systems View

HOW THRILLING IT is to live in this exciting time when human ingenuity knows no bounds. And how frightening too.

Beneath the veneer of shiny—urban centres light up in view of Earth-orbiting astronauts; the Olympian spirit on show every four years; virtually every tech convenience you can imagine—it all comes with a cost beyond what we can see. Our globe is warming, on a collision course with diminished futures. The growing gap between rich and poor is akin to the gap between what we know we ought to do and what we suppress, as though by some mass hypnosis we can't escape our inertia.

We need to gain a *systems view* of society and its values. We need to see the big picture. What is our society for? What is the basis of this collective? What is its systems goal? What do we all cherish? What do we all long for? Why not wish *every* person well? Why not cheer for *every child* in the global village?

Does business exist in a disconnected silo, or is it linked to communities? Do corporations have obligations? Is corporate social responsibility just a right-sounding phrase?

I've long felt that poisoning the Earth in the process of satisfying consumer wants is madness. It poisons our families. Think of it that way, as Ray Anderson did. He knew it was tantamount to poisoning tomorrow's children. We can choose a different path forward. We can heed the example of the organisms Janine Benyus describes, which "have figured out a way to do the amazing things they do while taking care of the place that's going to take care of their offspring."

Needs and wants are different things. And more than a century after Karl Marx made that point, once again we're at a time of choosing. Gandhi said the world has enough for our need, not for our greed. With 7 billion plus of us, headed for 9 billion by 2050, we can't ignore Gandhi's teaching.

• • •

The old European song "The More We Get Together" is *not* about social media. This first song on my first ever children's recording has been called "the social capital theme song" by Harvard economist Robert Putnam and UBC economist John Helliwell.[26] Why? Over 150 years, the song's essence has not been lost in translation. Putnam and Helliwell think that's because it speaks a truth: togetherness—real-life proximity—increases happiness, productivity and health. It's about sharing the benefits of joyful company, the resilient social fabric.

Radical rethink. If we can't have clean sustainable computing, what's the point? Is there a point to trashing the planet? One way or another, we are paying for our tech hubris. The cost of dirty electronics is very high.

"Everything at once," sings the new Windows TV ad. Clever slogan, dumb idea. With the human brain, everything at once won't work. The brain does what it has to do: filters out the noise at any given moment. That's what humanity has to do: lower the static so our higher purpose can shine.

Purpose. Relational wisdom. Maturity. That's the needed shift.

Sadly, money is the highest value in a global economy that ignores the social and environmental impacts of doing business. Economists call these "externalities," hard as that is to believe. Such a "bottom-line" corporate culture's approach to kids is not benign: it's to exploit them for profit. An economy with a triple bottom line—comprising fiscal, social and environmental responsibility—may not resemble the current global capitalism. So be it. Envision a *smart, sustaining economy*: one that cares, knows limits, restores as it provides.

With a Nature-oriented economy—a bionomy—we can rethink global consciousness. Nature rules, remember? Economy is a subset of Nature, as Ray Anderson said, not the other way round.

That's why monetizing every aspect of our lives—life as marketing, as branding—is, to my mind, the Midas Curse. Seeing everything in monetary terms is the Midas lust for gold. More money is the sole credo of this religion—more sales, more profit, more shareholder value, more return on investment (ROI).

Yet studies showing that society's greatest ROI is from investments in early childhood development go largely ignored. We still don't act on what we know: that early childhood is the *formative* period for a human life. One clear sign of a healthy, mature culture is that it recognizes this simple developmental truth.

When we design with the child in mind, all of society benefits.

Benign Design

THERE ARE RAYS of hope the world over. Benign by Design is an exciting concept for electronics manufacturing. Ted Smith describes it as a process in which, "at each stage of design and production of each component in a high tech device, we can ask, Are we using the most benign materials?"[27]

The Soesterberg Principles, adopted in 1999 by the Trans-Atlantic Network for Clean Production, wisely connect environmental, health and social issues in an integrated commitment for electronics sustainability: "Each new generation of technical improvements in electronic products should include parallel and proportional improvements in environmental, health and safety as well as social attributes."[28]

This key concept, which twins innovation with restoration, was adopted by the United Nations Strategic Approach to International Chemicals Management (SAICM) in Vienna in 2011. A report containing the Vienna recommendations includes four strategies for business and government:

1. Adopt green design, which promotes healthy systems for people and planet.
2. Know and disclose chemical and material ingredients.
3. Assess and avoid hazards by choosing safer materials.
4. Take responsibility from cradle to cradle (Extended Producer Responsibility).[29]

Extended Producer Responsibility (EPR), mentioned in the last point, puts the onus for full life-cycle responsibility—including the safe recycling and disassembly of products—on the manufacturer rather than the consumer. This is an example of CSR touted by sustainability advocates in other sectors: a "cradle to cradle" model of manufacturing in which consumers purchase merely the service benefits of a device, not the device itself. Thus, if there's a need to part with the device, under EPR, the manufacturer is responsible for what happens to it. This is a tidy, closed-loop system that can minimize waste—its goal is zero waste.

So what does this look like in the real world? Well, one example might be FairPhone.

Wait, did someone say *Fair*Phone?

The sprightly video at fairphone.com tells you that "FairPhone is the world's first collective non-profit technology company, developing a phone using minerals mined and sold under equity conditions." Admirable. The collective's mission is to market a smartphone designed and produced "with minimal harm to people and planet." Quick, someone tell Oprah! Isn't this the kind of "live your best life" venture she'd back? One that allows overseas smartphone labourers to also aspire? FairPhone claims are modest enough, not promising the sky just yet: "More ethically sourced, manufactured in better conditions and disposed of properly." If they can pull it off, *theirs* would be the *smart* phone.

Badphone, dirtyphone, darkphone: not quite a marketer's dream. FairPhone? Now we're getting somewhere.

Imagine: a phone made without the so-called conflict minerals that are a tragic but largely overlooked part of the InfoTech boom. Conflict minerals are those that "are mined and used to influence and finance armed conflict, human rights abuses, and violence."[30] In Congo, for example, the extraction of gold, tin, tantalum and tungsten, all found in consumer tech devices, has financed a decade-long war that has caused millions of deaths and is known for the widespread use of sexual assault against women as a weapon.[31] Growing public awareness spurred the US Congress to pass a law requiring that companies investigate to determine whether Congo conflict minerals are in their products' supply chains.[32]

For those who choose to look, listen and learn, the unsustainable features of the Darkweb become pretty clear. What we still need to develop and then implement is the sustainable pathway of the Lightweb that shows the way to a sustainable future. Barbara Kyle, Ted Smith and their colleagues at the Electronics TakeBack Coalition (ETBC) are working on a "Vision for Sustainable Electronics" (outlined on the following pages) that is not driven by monetary profit but, rather, is based on a broader, mature vision of what would profit people and the places where they live—a sustainability model with life-cycle goals.[33]

Such a vision could transform the electronics industry. And that would *dazzle the world all over again*.[34]

Vision for Sustainable Electronics

Current Situation (Problem)	Principles for Solutions: Vision for Sustainable Electronics
Hazards and harm • Toxic chemicals in products and production cause harm to workers (extraction, production and recycling workers), communities, environment and consumers. • Cost of using toxic material is externalized onto these groups.	**Materials and processes cause no harm** • At all lifecycle stages, materials and processes cause no harm to workers, communities, environments, ecosystems, or to users of the products. • Full disclosure of all materials throughout the lifecycle. • Zero hazardous or GHG [greenhouse gas] emissions. • Product price reflects true lifecycle costs.

Destruction of communities and resources • Activities destroy communities and sustainable economies (especially fishing, farming) by extreme pollution of water sources. • This is most common in mining, but also production and end of life. • Physical footprint not always at activity site, but downstream, downwind (mining, fracking). • Traditional lands altered forever—homes, livelihoods displaced (open-pit mining).	**Activities enrich communities** • Large-scale activities such as mining and manufacturing have a long-term positive impact on communities. • Must create long-term jobs, not just temporary mining jobs • Local populations (not just leaders) make decisions (free, prior, informed consent) about whether mine can be developed. • Adequate financial resources to protect the future.
Wasted resources: High consumption of energy and water • Extraction, production consume huge quantities of energy (non-renewable sources) and water (not reclaimed).	**Protection of natural resources** • Processes have low energy impacts and maximize use of renewable energy. • Processes have low water impacts and recycle all water. • Select and source materials where processes required to extract, process and recycle them use low amounts of energy. • Select and source materials where processes required to extract, process and recycle them use low amounts of water and recycle the water.
Wasteful churn of virgin materials, many of which are scarce • Manufacturing uses mostly virgin materials (in production and in product), not recycled materials. • Almost no closed loop recycling of materials or remanufacturing of products. • Inefficient processes create large amounts of waste—materials that are not easily recyclable, discharges. • Materials get lost in existing recovery processes, some still landfilled and incinerated.	**Sustainable inputs and outputs** • Processes use renewable materials that are infinitely recyclable without adding much new virgin content, and without down-cycling. • Circular economy: > Closed loop recycling of materials > Remanufacturing of products • Processes create zero waste. Waste = food, either food for the earth (compost) or "food" for manufacturing as industrial inputs. • Systems in place to fully recover and safely recycle all process and product outputs.

Sweatshop working conditions • Too much of the work (extraction, manufacturing, recycling) is done under sweatshop conditions in developing countries, where weak laws and lax enforcement don't protect people. • True costs are externalized to workers, communities in these countries.	**Safe and fair working conditions** • Workers make a living wage, and labor under healthy, safe and fair conditions. • True production costs are internalized into the price of the product.
Business model makes problems worse • Primary metric is quarterly earnings. • Products designed to be obsolete, replaced with new. • Design focus only on product performance, not on lifecycle impacts.	**New business models prioritize sustainability, embrace lifecycle goals** • Companies are as accountable to sustainability goals as to quarterly profits goals. • Businesses report on long-term sustainability strategies. • All costs are internalized, so customers pay true costs.

Source: Under development by Electronics TakeBack Coalition (ETBC). Used with permission of Barbara Kyle, Ted Smith and ETBC.

• • •

The three reasons for critically needed social media reform—safety, intelligence, sustainability—exist in a holarchy in which one feeds and supports the other. If safety by design can reform SM to be safe for young users, that certainly would enhance their ability to use social networks wisely, which can support and enhance their inherent intelligence and thus make InfoTech use a sustainable and sustaining practice.

Benign with the child in mind. A vision for humanity.

"If we change the beginning of the story, we change the whole story."[35]

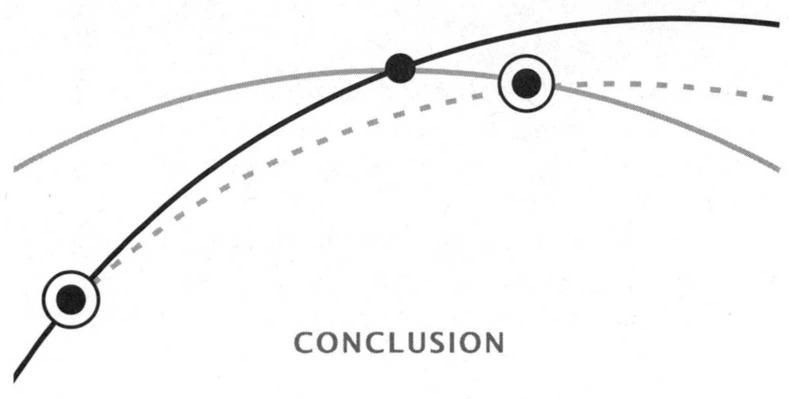

CONCLUSION

There can be no keener revelation of a society's soul than the way in which it treats its children.

~ Nelson Mandela

SAFE, INTELLIGENT, SUSTAINABLE. That's precisely what our species needs of any new revolutionary technology—especially innovation that affects our young and might shape the fabric of society for generations to come.

In the rapid rise of the much-touted digital revolution, the safety of young social media users was an afterthought. The emotional intelligence impact—in anti-social and addictive behaviours—on frequent visitors to the lawless cyber frontier was ignored by InfoTech's profit-driven expansion. And, as is common in "business as usual," the unsustainable means for bringing digital devices to market lay hidden. Unsafe, ill-considered, unsustainable: hardly the makings of digital utopia.

While it's true that one can be well-informed via SM, it's also true that the Net's info glut can give users a social and cognitive disorientation that's hard to measure. At a time when humanity needs to be at its best and smartest—to see the big picture—we're profoundly distracted by triviality.

My aim in this small book was to ask questions not asked, to provoke thought and discussion, and to deepen the conversation on a technology that most influences young users and may have generational consequences.

For the Information Superhighway, this book might provide the "power brakes" that allow more precise "power steering" for where you wish to go, and for getting there safely.

• • •

An acute awareness of both the light and dark sides of InfoTech is critical if we are to counter its addictive power and vast overreach. The capacity for critical thinking, for what I call "radical inquiry," is needed now more than ever. As Evgeny Morozov writes in *The Net Delusion*:

> By adopting a deterministic stance, we are less likely to subject technology—and those who make a living from it—to the full bouquet of ethical questions normal for democracy. Should Google be required to encrypt all documents uploaded to its Google Docs service? Should Facebook be allowed to continue making more of their users' data public? Should Twitter be invited to high-profile gatherings of the US government without first signing up with the Global Network Initiative?...
>
> ...The growing disconnect between Silicon Valley's reluctance to accept the social responsibility that comes with the ownership of today's digital public squares and the glowing public admiration these companies receive is one more reason to take a more critical stance and examine the cultural origins of our benevolent attitudes toward these corporate titans.[1]

Please Remember

IF DIGITAL TECH has quickly cast us in a hypnotic state, the roots of that trance lie in previous decades during which many hopes were dashed—hopes of breakthroughs on many issues, a list that would include transcending fossil fuel dependency, cleaning up toxic supersites, curbing corporate abuses (think Wall Street), and addressing climate change.

How many surveys, studies and reports can humanity ignore on the key integrated issue of planetary and social health? We've had warnings galore, for decades. Failure to act is what grows anxiety. Knowing what we must do as a society and yet not doing it, that grows cynicism. Remember the Occupy movement?

Why will we not act? Partly because we live in an economic model that rewards short-termism. And partly because the rise of corporate power muzzles reasonable dissent in favour of the bottom line.

We can't say we didn't know; we were warned. Think Aldous Huxley, and George Orwell. Think of Charlie Chaplin in the 1940 film *The Great Dictator*:

> We all want to help one another. Human beings are like that. We want to live by each other's happiness, not by each other's misery. We don't want to hate and despise one another. In this world there is room for everyone. And the good Earth is rich and can provide for everyone. The way of life can be free and beautiful, but we have lost the way.
>
> Our knowledge has made us cynical; our cleverness, hard and unkind. We think too much and feel too little. More than machinery, we need humanity. More than cleverness, we need kindness and gentleness. Without these qualities, life will be violent and all will be lost.[2]

A timeless classic, an appeal that could well have been written for today's world. These words can haunt us, and they can inspire us to higher purpose.

World War II. Hiroshima and Nagasaki. The Cold War.

US President Eisenhower's 1961 farewell address was a stern warning about the excesses of power. "America's leadership and prestige depend...on how we use our power in the interests of world peace and human betterment," Eisenhower said. He went on, "In the councils of government, we must guard against the acquisition of unwarranted influence, whether sought or unsought, by the military-industrial complex."

The following year, Rachel Carson's book *Silent Spring* launched the environmental movement.[3]

In 1977, Marie Winn's book *The Plug-In Drug* sounded an early alarm on "TV addiction in children." In 1983 she published *Children Without Childhood*, a book that warned us about the overstimulated child hurtling to adulthood.[4] Neil Postman's 1985 book *Amusing Ourselves to Death* outlined the TV-led media makeover of rational discourse as entertainment.[5]

As early as 1989, David Suzuki referred to global warming as "a matter of survival."[6] Then came Bill McKibben's books *Enough* and *The End of Nature*.[7] Al Gore's 1991 book *Earth in the Balance* proposed that ecology become society's central organizing principle.[8]

1992 brought the "World Scientists' Warning To Humanity" from the US-based Union of Concerned Scientists, a warning that got little to no media attention.[9] Who now can remember that report?

Also in 1992, at the UN Earth Summit in Rio de Janeiro, conference secretary-general Maurice Strong warned of the urgent need to embrace sustainability: "Frankly, we may get to the point where the only way of saving the world will be for industrial civilization to collapse."[10]

In 1993, I was in Japan at the Kyoto Global Forum, and I heard Mikhail Gorbachev speak on Earth Day on the conference theme, "Value Change for Global Survival." (It's worth mentioning here that not only did Gorbachev's *glasnost* and *perestroika*—openness and restructuring—unravel the mighty Soviet Union, but after the Chernobyl nuclear disaster he turned into an ecology advocate.) In his plenary address, Gorbachev said: "The problem of saving planet Earth is, in fact, the main problem. It has absolute priority among all other problems facing humankind today." That was in 1993. And it's still absolutely relevant. Where are the state leaders who speak such words today?

Have we really forgotten the warnings? Or has corporate power made them irrelevant? The great irony here is that on the Internet you can find the most stirring and courageous speeches of Martin Luther King Jr and of Nelson Mandela. You can be inspired by the likes of Jane Goodall. You can find endless sources of inspiration. But first, you must want to.

In a recent essay, "The Right to a Future," I wrote the following:

> In a well-known Greek myth, the very rich King Midas, who loves gold above all else, is granted his singular wish that everything he touches turn into gold. The gift becomes a curse when his golden touch kills plants, food, and even his daughter, who is turned into a statue. Bereft and repentant, forsaking greed, the king begs for deliverance. His curse is lifted by a wash in the river. All he holds truly precious is restored.
>
> The modern version of the story is about a gold rush called globalization, a monetized world order that commodifies everything and poisons all that it touches: air, water, soil, whales, indigenous cultures, mothers' milk, and babies, now born with a body burden of toxic chemicals. Money as symbolic reward for goods and services, when elevated above all else, becomes a curse. The symbol turns tyrant and casts a plague on the living. We're currently in the atonement chapter of the tragedy, praying we have time to write a happier ending.[11]

Gorbachev's "value change" comes to mind. *Glasnost, perestroika*. Openness, restructuring: what we must demand of SM providers.

Response Ability

DURING THE RESEARCH phase of this book, I learned a great deal about the light and dark sides of InfoTech. I learned much more about the Darkweb than I cared to, and that brought much anguish to the writing process. As for the open letter to Facebook COO Sheryl Sandberg in the wake of Amanda Todd's suicide—no response.

The silence had been deafening. Another youth has taken her life.

Six months after the Todd tragedy, 17-year-old Rehtaeh Parsons died in hospital after a suicide attempt in Halifax, Nova Scotia. Her mother said that Rehtaeh, when she was 15, had been raped by four high school students. Images of that assault had been shared via SM and propelled a torrent of online abuse towards Rehtaeh, as if *she* was somehow to blame for the horrific crime.

There was a huge public outcry, and after an online petition was signed by over 400,000 Canadians, an independent inquiry was established to examine the original police investigation that brought no charges against the alleged perpetrators.[12] The premier of Nova Scotia has called for changes in Canada's criminal code to ensure legislation keeps pace with the disturbing emergence of online violence.[13]

From Steubenville, Ohio, and San Jose, California, came news of other teen sexual assaults and online shamings, the California case ending with the suicide of Audrie Pott. It's hard to foresee how long this tech-enabled criminal vulgarity can continue.

What we can imagine is the possibility that in a few short years SM's bubble may have burst, or at least Facebook's. Already there are reports of teens switching to newer platforms,[14] and recent news stories describe advertisers' dismay that their ads are posted on disgusting FB pages with photos of rape and other vile content.[15]

• • •

Sad to say, social media's known security gaps present a clear and present danger to young users, and its addictive allure brings a new behavioural challenge to families and to society as a whole.

There is no new model of early child development to justify the aggressive marketing of infant and toddler apps for tablets and even smartphones. The widespread proliferation of InfoTech tablets, and the rush by parents to use them as babysitting pacifiers, brings a serious disruption to early childhood, and we have no evidence that it provides any benefit. If social media is addictive, and we know it is, the compulsion to instant push-button gratification from an early age is not something we can afford.[16] And yet many parents are unthinkingly putting shiny tech devices in their little kids' hands.

Perhaps most worrisome is an April 23, 2013, article in the *Tokyo Times* informing us of a new private social network for 2- to 7-year-olds in China, similar to Facebook.[17] Described as a "mobile education platform," SmarTots allows little kids to share their art-work, and lets parents and grandparents "like" it. An irony here is that, left to their own devices (pun intended), little ones early in life have the most fun and learn best through active real-world play, and by using crayons, markers, and paints and brushes when they draw. Widespread tech disruption of such early year conventions is unprecedented. Child development professionals might call this intrusion into early childhood reckless and unwarranted. I would agree.

• • •

In late March 2013, a baby girl was born to my niece Kristin and her husband, Ivan, and so I became a great-uncle. In the joy of marvelling at this home birth and welcoming little Lucie to the world, I paused to imagine the wonders she would behold in her life. Her parents have asked friends and family to respect their desire to keep a "low digital profile" for her in terms of online photos. This is something all parents might choose for their kids; it retains a degree of privacy for birth announcements, which are, after all, not usually broadcast to the whole world.

I pray that Lucie may know a world in which her online safety is assured. I pray that elected leaders will act quickly to bring some regulation to the lawless Internet to curb the current dark-side perils. I pray that the emotional intelligence of society will hasten the chance for everyone to use the Lightweb for good.

Respecting Earth and Child

WILL PEOPLE ONE day realize that we need to honour the real world but find that it's too late and there are too few left who know how?

We pre-digital adults are custodians of a real world our children may not know or remember. If future parents have not known a pre-digital life, how will they maintain optimal balance between the real and virtual worlds? We, then, have a solemn duty to know, remember and teach vital real-world qualities to the young.

Ecology and children have been my twin passions throughout my adult life. In my work with the Centre for Child Honouring, it became abundantly clear that what humanity needs is to *simultaneously* respect Mother Nature and her children (all of them), and that, everywhere, this respect would ensure the best possible society.

People dream of a better world for their children. This universal dream is rooted in the hope of progress. But hopes repeatedly dashed can breed cynicism, the cousin of dysfunction and violence.

For many decades our world has suffered offensive technologies too numerous to mention: nuclear warheads, highly toxic industrial chemicals and practices, strip mining and ocean-floor trawling come to mind. Yet most families were not directly involved in creating or doing these things. That changes with digital technology—it has befriended our young, its current is in their heads, and its daily worldwide use votes in its favour.

How then can we keep the Lightweb while reducing the Darkweb? How do we use this technology with minimal harm? How do we tilt the risk-benefit ratio towards respecting Earth and Child?

• • •

For societies to mature, they must invest in the conditions that enable their citizens to mature. They need the emotional infrastructure that enables and encourages their young to come of age. Healthy individuation is the way to responsible adulthood, the way to grow mature persons engaged with and contributing to society.

Unhealthy enculturation comes from a culture stuck in arrested development, one that does not progress along its maturing human potential, one in which the priorities are all wrong: a culture that values money above all else, glorifies violence and sexualizes its young, for example. Namely, our bully culture.

Healthy individuation rests on many factors, most importantly a loving start to life: in pregnancy, birthing and the formative first years of bonding and attachment. And as we grow we need the continuum of belonging to a loving village.[18]

Peaceful resistance to *unhealthy* enculturation is the work required of the entire global village, every person, rooted in universal virtues of love and nurturance, brave enough to not feign allegiance to the life-destroying practices of patriarchy and its monetary bottom line.

Beyond Social Media

THE LIGHTWEB BENEFITS of social networks and the InfoTech that brings them to our hands are well known. Lesser known are the downsides. Currently the Darkweb casts too large and negative a shadow on InfoTech users, especially the young.

Safety
loss of privacy, identity theft, cyberbullying, sexting, online shaming, predatory victimizing, wireless radiation

Intelligence
dependency, addiction, conversation phobia, lack of exercise, weight gain, anxiety, sleep disruption, reduced contemplation, inability to be alone, obsessive virtuality, false intimacy, undeveloped capacity for vulnerability, prevalence of pornography

Sustainability
product obsolescence, e-waste, rare earth minerals extraction, toxic mining processes, damage to workers' health (in mining, manufacturing, recycling)

Can you see why we can't optimize or enjoy the benefits of the Lightweb without constraining the Darkweb? Can you see that the cost of not reforming social media is too high?

We are at a crossroads as a civilization.

Compulsive social media use by the young compromises their security, alters their brains and undermines family time. InfoTech titans sell new tech drugs to ever-dependent buyers. Cyber enthusiasts envision teacherless touch-screen learning as the future of education.

A handful of billionaires and their tech companies race to rewire the human future with hardly a thought as to what's best for children. The societal "lovelessness" that Huxley wrote about is promoted as progress to a populace dumbed down by excessive screen time and pacified by excessive information.[19] Profiteers willfully market to kids video games designed to be addictive.[20]

An unhealthy culture cannot generate wellbeing in the populace. Here's another recent sign of trouble.

To market a new feature called Facebook Home, FB's TV ad called "Dinner" pits a teenage girl against a dinner guest (or family member) who is boring her. She finds refuge in her smartphone, which takes her out of her apparently intolerable situation. With this ad, Zuckerberg, Sandberg and company are tearing at the fabric of society, pitting young against old in an ad that's anti-family, anti-social, anti-home. Such is the corporate greed that targets our kids.

Resisting this loveless, unhealthy culture is not an option—it is our human duty.

Just as humanity has crossed a threshold in its relational onslaught on Nature, we seem poised to violate (with virtuality) the innocence, energy and spirit of another realm: childhood. Reason to pause, rethink, refresh.

Reclaim the real.

The true ground of our being is nested within family and community that births us, and within Nature that sustains us. Ground yourself in the real. Now, more than ever, know your roots.

Wisdom stories of our ancestors, wisdom of indigenous peoples: these legacies are the indispensable riches of our lives. Know your roots in the circle of human belonging. Honour the magic of Creation.

Curb the Darkweb. Enjoy the Lightweb.

This world encyclopedia at your fingertips: may you use it safely, wisely, and always for good.

Appendix A: Making the Best of It

"First, Do No Harm," the physician's oath, can apply to all areas of life, including InfoTech.

When we think about how families can make the best of a very challenging social media landscape—how we can subdue the Darkweb and thus enjoy the Lightweb—consider the safety, intelligence and sustainability costs of the Darkweb, outlined on page 130.

There are many things you can do to safeguard your own and your children's online experience and ensure that InfoTech does not become an obsession or addiction. Here are some suggestions:

- Join Red Hood Project, a movement for online safety for young users. Visit the website at redhoodproject.com, sign the Open Letter to Facebook, and click on the What Can You Do button.
- Join the global movement to honour the child. Visit the Centre for Child Honouring website (childhonouring.org) and download the Covenant and Principles. Take them to heart.
- Have a family policy to keep shiny tech devices out of kids' bedrooms at night.
- Make your family meals and get-togethers screen-free zones.
- Have at least one day a week be a screen-free day.
- Take an occasional break from social media; better yet, take a regular SM fast.
- Make sure your home phone and Internet connections are wired, not wireless. To reduce microwave radiation in your surroundings, minimize cellphone use, and keep smartphones on the Airplane Mode setting at night.
- Support green electronics initiatives and coalitions. Read the book *Challenging the Chip* and watch the video *The Story of Electronics* with your children.
- When you recycle your used electronics, use an E-Stewards

certified recycler. See their website (e-stewards.org) to locate one near you.

Parents: please remember—InfoTech can wait!

- Childhood is precious; the early years fly by. Your kids will have the rest of their lives for engaging InfoTech.
- As shiny tech is so easy to use (and changes every six months), there's no need to start kids young. InfoTech is easy at any age.
- The best advantage you can give little kids is your presence in their lives. Also books, songs, the arts, active play, the outdoors.
- Do not use shiny tech as a pacifier or babysitter.
- Say NO to violent video games.
- Teach children basic mindfulness meditation. Start them doing 5 minutes per day and then increase to 10 minutes.
- Cellphones are not needed until the teen years. And when your teens get one, make sure it has minimal texting and phone service. Let them pay for it themselves.
- Smartphones can wait until your teen is old enough to drive on the Information Superhighway (age 16) and has a licence—that is, a good understanding of digital citizenship and literacy.

Common Sense Media has a comprehensive Digital Citizenship and Literacy curriculum for K-12 (commonsensemedia.org). Parents or teachers can visit the website, click on Educators, then Curriculum, and choose among various grade levels to help children develop their digital citizenship and literacy skills for the online world.

The idea of digital citizenship and literacy is gaining momentum. Digital citizenship teaches that when we are online, we should accord people the same courtesy and respect we'd give them in the real world. It also reminds us that we are accountable for what we do online. Digital literacy teaches us about InfoTech issues so we can avoid the Darkweb's dangers.

Appendix B: Red Hood Project

Posted on Red Hood Project website, April 4, 2013:
http://www.redhoodproject.com/red-hood-project-statement-of-objectives/

The parameters around child protection online are overwhelming and constantly changing. However, as a starting point, Red Hood Project proposes four minimum standards:

1. Age verification
2. Disabled location and web browser tracking
3. Default privacy/app settings
4. Firewall protection for children's data online

Introduction: Data protection

Children have an inherent and special right to privacy preservation.

We have entered a new era in which both social media and other corporate entities gather a vast array of our personal data, and it's impossible to predict or even know what use will be made of it.

This makes a mockery of informed consent, and is especially problematic for children's data. Relying on parents alone to manage this issue leaves far too many children vulnerable. Many parents cannot keep up with technology. Even those who inform themselves will be out of date within weeks.

Because of the unpredictability of our online future and the clear trend toward invasion of privacy, we should preserve children's data privacy until they are old enough to make informed choices for themselves.

1. Age verification

There can be no specialized protection of children's privacy rights without verification of who is a child.

Identity and age verification is much more common than we generally imagine. Banking, credit card, and PayPal sites all provide enhanced security protections and require identity verification. Children should be as safe online as our credit cards.

Red Hood Project calls for social media and online providers to know when account holders are children. This will probably be easiest to achieve through mobile phones, as almost all smartphones are provided to children by parents, giving mobile providers a responsible adult point of contact.

As child online users migrate to smartphones, society has a unique opportunity to capture this moment and establish necessary protections through mobile providers.

2. Disabled location tracking and web browser tracking

(a) Location tracking

GPS location tracking enabled by smartphone technology allows users to be located within 10 meters. People with this information don't only know where children live; they can determine their physical movements and habits. They know when kids are at soccer practice or a concert. They may be able to tell when they are home alone.

As a matter of personal safety, it should not be possible to physically locate anyone online (without their consent). This especially pertains to children. Senator Al Franken in the US has taken a strong leadership position, seeking to disable all location tracking. Learn more at http://www.alfranken.com/pages/consumers_privacy_netneutrality

(b) Web browser tracking

Tracking of web browser behaviour is a multi-billion-dollar industry. As Gary Kovacs, CEO of Mozilla, outlined in his TED talk,[1] even young children visiting websites with children's content are tracked by dozens of unseen sites that monetize their behaviour. It's wrong to track children's behaviour. Society, including our corporate sector, has an obligation to protect their privacy.

3. Default privacy settings for children and youth

Instagram, owned by Facebook, is one example of potential hazards and dangers to children, who can too easily inadvertently disclose their home address, cell-phone numbers, and even physical location.

The ideal circumstance would be for social media and mobile providers to provide children and youth with default settings that prevent public disclosure of identity information.

4. Firewall protection for children online

Red Hood Project advocates that children online be protected from unwelcome monitoring, surveillance, and communication from strangers. No adult should be able to follow, track or communicate with a child they do not know.

Social media corporations have an obligation to provide advanced security protections that safeguard children from known threats.

Appendix C: Is the Internet Hurting Children?

Posted on the CNN website, May 21, 2012:
http://www.cnn.com/2012/05/21/opinion/clinton-steyer-internet-kids

Editor's note: *Chelsea Clinton is a board member of Common Sense Media, a nonprofit advocacy organization focused on media and technology's effects on children and teens, and wrote the foreword to "Talking Back to Facebook." James P. Steyer is founder and CEO of Common Sense Media and the author of "Talking Back to Facebook."*

(CNN)— Amid the buzz over the Facebook IPO, the ever-evolving theories about how Twitter is reshaping our communications and speculation about where the next social media-enabled protest or revolution will occur, there is an important question we've largely ignored. What are the real effects of all this on the huge segment of the population most affected by social media themselves: our children and our teens?

The explosive growth of social media, smartphones and digital devices is transforming our kids' lives, in school and at home. Research tells us that even the youngest of our children are migrating online, using tablets and smartphones, downloading apps. Consumer Reports reported last year that more than 7.5 million American kids under the age of 13 have joined Facebook, which technically requires users to be 13 years old to open an account. No one has any idea of what all of this media and technology use will mean for our kids as they grow up.

By the time they're 2 years old, more than 90% of all American children have an online history. At 5, more than 50% regularly interact with a computer or tablet device, and by 7 or 8, many kids regularly play video games. Teenagers text an average of 3,400 times a month. The fact is, by middle school, our kids today are spending more time with media than with their parents or teachers, and the challenges are vast: from the millions of young people who regret by high school what they've already posted about themselves online to the widely documented rise in cyberbullying to the hypersexualization of female characters in video games.

These challenges also include traditional media and the phenomenon of "ratings creep" in the movies that our kids consume. Movies today—even G-rated ones—contain significantly more sex and violence, on average, than movies with the same rating 10 or 20 years ago.

The impact of heavy media and technology use on kids' social, emotional and cognitive development is only beginning to be studied, and the emergent results are serious. While the research is still in its early stages, it suggests that the Internet may actually be changing how our brains work. Too much hypertext and multimedia content has been linked in some kids to limited attention span, lower comprehension, poor focus, greater risk for depression and diminished long-term memory.

Our new world of digital immersion and multitasking has affected virtually everything from our thought processes and work habits to our capacity for linear thinking and how we feel about ourselves, our friends and even strangers. And it has all happened virtually overnight.

It goes without saying that digital media have also altered our fundamental notions of and respect for privacy. Young people now routinely post and share private, personal information and opinions on social media platforms without fully considering the potential consequences.

The immediacy of social media platforms, coupled with vulnerable youngsters who are socially inexperienced and not fully developed emotionally, can create a combustible mix. Kids often self-reveal before they reflect, and millions of kids say and do things they later regret. The permanence of what anyone posts online and the absence of an "eraser" button mean that the embarrassment and potential damage can last forever.

We urgently need a public conversation in our country among key stakeholders: parents, educators, technology innovators, policymakers and young people themselves. The dialogue must focus on the ways social media and technology enable our kids to give up their privacy before they fully understand what privacy is and why it's important to all of us. We should also discuss how social media can help empower kids to find their voice, find their purpose and potentially create the next technology revolution.

All adults know that the teen years are a critical time for identity exploration and experimentation. Yet this important developmental phase can be dramatically twisted when that identity experimentation, however personal and private, appears permanently on one's digital record for all to see.

In the 1990s, as a reaction to an explosion of television programming of increasingly questionable quality for kids, Congress passed the Children's Television Act. There was universal recognition that given all the time kids were spending in front of the television, the nation had a collective responsibility to offer positive, educational programming with limited commercials. We are at, arguably, an even more important crossroads when it comes to digital media and technology.

Howard Gardner, a professor and researcher at the Harvard Graduate School of Education who developed the concept of multiple intelligences, calls kids' use of digital media and technology "epochal change." He compares the revolution in digital media to the invention of the printing press because of its extraordinary impact on the way we communicate, share information and interact with one another. As a society, we have no choice but to engage with this new reality and work to ensure that it affects our kids in healthy, responsible ways.

The promise of digital media to transform our lives in positive ways is enormous. If managed well, technology can improve our schools and education, deepen social connectedness, expand civic engagement and even help advance our democracy. But for these positive outcomes to occur, we as a society must confront the challenges endemic in our 24/7 digital world.

We need legislation, educational efforts and norms that reflect 21st-century realities to maximize the opportunities and minimize the risks for our kids. Only then will we be able to give them the safe, healthy childhood and adolescence they deserve.

Appendix D: Recommendations and Comments

I want to bring your attention to a selection of recommendations and comments from a number of prominent individuals and organizations on the global phenomenon affecting every continent: the InfoTech revolution.

What follows is focused on parental responsibility, for the home is (or should be) where children primarily get their guidance.

Jim Steyer, CEO of Common Sense Media, a US organization with a rich online resource of media advice, is an outspoken champion of common sense and active parenting when it comes to digital technology. Steyer's book *Talking Back to Facebook: The Common Sense Guide to Raising Kids in the Digital Age* is indispensable for parents.[1]

In a TV interview in 2012, Steyer nicely summed up his advice for parents:

1. Set firm time limits.
2. Choose age-appropriate material.
3. Unplug.
4. Learn their world.
5. Keep computers in a common area.

Advice from many quarters confirms the wisdom of this approach to setting limits for kids' distraction, understanding the importance of privacy and grounding their formative experience in the real world.

In April 2010, **Marc Rotenberg** of EPIC (Electronic Privacy Information Center) testified before the US Senate Subcommittee on Consumer Protection, Product Safety, and Insurance.[2] He was speaking about the Children's Online Privacy Protection Act (COPPA), enacted in 1998 and now dealing with the profusion of new social media sites:

Today, I recommend that Congress raise the age requirement in COPPA to 18. The emergence of social networks and the powerful commercial forces that are seeking to extract personal data on all users of these services, but particularly children, raise new challenges that the original COPPA simply did not contemplate...

If the Congress chooses not to raise the age on COPPA, then I anticipate that the privacy problems will grow more severe in the next few years. Not only will companies that target young teens gather more data, their business practices will become increasingly more opaque and more difficult for users to manage. We have seen just in the last few years how companies such as Facebook have found that they can manipulate privacy settings and change privacy policies to coax personal information out of users who had earlier made clear which information they would reveal and which information they would keep private.

Dr Ann Cavoukian, Privacy Commissioner, Office of Information and Privacy, Ontario:

Calls for the imminent death of privacy are fatally flawed. The massive growth of online social networks has led some to believe that there can be no privacy in the future: the more people connect, the less privacy we can have, right? Wrong! This type of classic zero-sum thinking is inherently flawed and should be exposed for the folly it represents. Not only can we have both social contact AND privacy, we must have both.

As a social psychologist, I well recognize that we are social animals who love to connect with others. But I also recognize that the human condition seeks out time for reflection, reserve, solitude, and intimacy— all of which are predicated on privacy.

We must have both social contact and privacy, and we can indeed have both. Humans are capable of enjoying multiple states of being

> and experiencing different facets of contact—this is called a positive sum, not zero-sum, paradigm, where multiple conditions may be positively experienced in unison. We can and must have both social contact and privacy—the human condition requires both.[3]

In 2003 the **Canadian Paediatric Society** prepared a position statement on media use and children.[4] It included the following comments:

> *The dangers inherent in this relatively uncontrolled "wired" world are many and varied, but often hidden.* [italics mine] These dangers must be unmasked and a wise parent will learn how to protect their children by immersing themselves in the medium and taking advice from the many resources aimed at protecting children while allowing them to reap the rich benefits in a safe environment...
>
> Other concerns include pedophiles who use the Internet to lure young people into relationships. There is also the potential for children to be exposed to pornographic material. Parents can use technology that blocks access to pornography and sex talk on the Internet, but must be aware that this technology does not replace their supervision or guidance.
>
> There is a wealth of information on coping with the vast resources of the Web, both good and bad. Above all, parents should be encouraged to appreciate that there is potential for more good than bad, *as long as one has the knowledge to tell the difference.* [italics mine]...
>
> - Families should be encouraged to explore media together and discuss their educational value. Children should be encouraged to criticize and analyze what they see in the media. Parents can help children differentiate between fantasy and reality, particularly when it comes to sex, violence and advertising.
> - No child should be allowed to have a television, computer or video game equipment in his or her bedroom. A central loca-

tion is strongly advised with common access and common passwords.

- Television watching should be limited to less than 1 h to 2 h per day. Families may want to consider more active and creative ways to spend time together.
- Older children should be offered an opportunity to make choices by planning the week's viewing schedule in advance. Ideally, parents should supervise these choices and be good role models by making their own wise choices. Parents should explain why some programs are not suitable and praise children for making good and appropriate choices.
- Families should limit the use of television, computers or video games as a diversion, substitute teacher or electronic nanny. Parents should also ask alternative caregivers to maintain the same rules for media use in their absence. The rules in divorced parents' households should be consistent.

In 2011, the **American Academy of Pediatrics** published an article on social media and children, adolescents and family in its official journal. The authors cover some benefits of the Lightweb but also take a good look at the Darkweb. What follows is an abridged version of the article, reproduced with permission; the full document is available online.[5]

Benefits of Children and Adolescents Using Social Media

Socialization and Communication

Social media sites allow teens to accomplish online many of the tasks that are important to them offline: staying connected with friends and family, making new friends, sharing pictures, and exchanging ideas. Social media participation also can offer adolescents deeper benefits that extend into their view of self, community, and the world, including:

- opportunities for community engagement through raising money for charity and volunteering for local events, including political and philanthropic events;
- enhancement of individual and collective creativity through development and sharing of artistic and musical endeavors;
- growth of ideas from the creation of blogs, podcasts, videos, and gaming sites;
- expansion of one's online connections through shared interests to include others from more diverse backgrounds (such communication is an important step for all adolescents and affords the opportunity for respect, tolerance, and increased discourse about personal and global issues); and
- fostering of one's individual identity and unique social skills.

Enhanced Learning Opportunities

Middle and high school students are using social media to connect with one another on homework and group projects. For example, Facebook and similar social media programs allow students to gather outside of class to collaborate and exchange ideas about assignments. Some schools successfully use blogs as teaching tools, which has the benefit of reinforcing skills in English, written expression, and creativity.

Accessing Health Information

Adolescents are finding that they can access online information about their health concerns easily and anonymously. Excellent health resources are increasingly available to youth on a variety of topics of interest to this population, such as sexually transmitted infections, stress reduction, and signs of depression. Adolescents with chronic illnesses can access Web sites through which they can develop supportive networks of people with similar conditions. The mobile technologies that teens use daily, namely cell phones, instant messaging, and text messaging, have already produced multiple improvements in their health care, such as increased medication adherence, better disease understanding, and fewer missed appointments. Given that the new social media venues all have mobile applications, teenagers will have enhanced opportunities to learn about their health issues and communicate with their doctors.

However, because of their young age, adolescents can encounter inaccuracies during these searches and require parental involvement to be sure they are using reliable online resources, interpreting the information correctly, and not becoming overwhelmed by the information they are reading...

Risks of Youth Using Social Media

Using social media becomes a risk to adolescents more often than most adults realize. Most risks fall into the following categories: peer-to-peer; inappropriate content; lack of understanding of online privacy issues; and outside influences of third-party advertising groups.

Cyberbullying and Online Harassment

Cyberbullying is deliberately using digital media to communicate false, embarrassing, or hostile information about another person. It is the most common online risk for all teens and is a peer-to-peer risk.

Although "online harassment" is often used interchangeably with the term "cyberbullying," it is actually a different entity. Current data suggest that online harassment is not as common as offline harassment, and participation in social networking sites does not put most children at risk of online harassment. On the other hand, cyberbullying is quite common, can occur to any young person online, and can cause profound psychosocial outcomes including depression, anxiety, severe isolation, and, tragically, suicide.

Sexting

Sexting can be defined as "sending, receiving, or forwarding sexually explicit messages, photographs, or images via cell phone, computer, or other digital devices." Many of these images become distributed rapidly via cell phones or the Internet. This phenomenon does occur among the teen population; a recent survey revealed that 20% of teens have sent or posted nude or seminude photographs or videos of themselves. Some teens who have engaged in sexting have been threatened or charged with felony child pornography charges, although some states have started characterizing such behaviors as juvenile-law misdemeanors. Additional consequences include school suspension for perpetrators and emotional distress with accompanying mental health conditions for victims. In many circumstances, however, the sexting incident is not shared beyond a small peer group or a couple and is not found to be distressing at all.

Facebook Depression

Researchers have proposed a new phenomenon called "Facebook depression," defined as depression that develops when preteens and teens spend a great deal of time on social media sites, such as Facebook, and then begin to exhibit classic symptoms of depression. Acceptance by and contact with peers is an important element of adolescent life. The intensity of the online world is thought to be a factor that may trigger depression in some adolescents. As with offline depression, preadolescents and adolescents who suffer from Facebook depression are at risk for social isolation and sometimes turn to risky Internet sites and blogs for "help" that may promote substance abuse, unsafe sexual practices, or aggressive or self-destructive behaviors.

Privacy Concerns and the Digital Footprint

The main risks to preadolescents and adolescents online today are risks from each other, risks of improper use of technology, lack of privacy, sharing too much information, or posting false information about themselves or others. These types of behavior put their privacy at risk.

When Internet users visit various Web sites, they can leave behind evidence of which sites they have visited. This collective, ongoing record of one's Web activity is called the "digital footprint." One of the biggest threats to young people on social media sites is to their digital footprint and future reputations. Preadolescents and adolescents who lack an awareness of privacy issues often post inappropriate messages, pictures, and videos without understanding that "what goes online stays online." As a result, future jobs and college acceptance may be put into jeopardy by inexperienced and rash clicks of the mouse. Indiscriminate Internet activity also can make children and teenagers easier for marketers and fraudsters to target.

Influence of Advertisements on Buying

Many social media sites display multiple advertisements such as banner ads, behavior ads (ads that target people on the basis of their Web-browsing behavior), and demographic-based ads (ads that target people on the basis of a specific factor such as age, gender, education, marital status, etc.) that influence not only the buying tendencies of preadolescents and adolescents but also their views of what is normal. It is particularly important for parents to be aware of the behavioral ads, because they are common on social media sites and operate by gathering information on the person using a site and then targeting that person's profile to influence purchasing decisions. Such powerful influences start as soon as children begin to go online and post. Many online venues are now prohibiting ads on sites where children and adolescents are participating. It is important to educate parents, children, and adolescents about this practice so that children can develop into media-literate consumers and understand how advertisements can easily manipulate them.

On Too Young: Mixed Messages from Parents and the Law

Many parents are aware that 13 years is the minimum age for most social media sites but do not understand why. There are 2 major reasons. First, 13 years is the age set by Congress in the Children's Online Privacy Protection Act (COPPA), which prohibits Web sites from collecting information on children younger than 13 years without parental permission. Second, the official terms of service for many popular sites now mirror the COPPA regulations and state that 13 years is the minimum age to sign up and have a profile. This is the minimum age to sign on to sites such as Facebook and MySpace. There are many sites for preadolescents and younger children that do not have such an age restriction, such as Disney sites, Club Penguin, and others.

It is important that parents evaluate the sites on which their child wishes to participate to be sure that the site is appropriate for that child's age. For sites without age stipulations, however, there is room for negotiation, and parents should evaluate the situation via active conversation with their preadolescents and adolescents.

In general, if a Web site specifies a minimum age for use in its terms of service, the American Academy of Pediatrics (AAP) encourages that age to be respected. Falsifying age has become common practice by some preadolescents and some parents. Parents must be thoughtful about this practice to be sure that they are not sending mixed messages about lying and that online safety is always the main message being emphasized.

ACKNOWLEDGMENTS

For conversations that nourished the writing of this book, I thank Sabrina Aven, Adela Barcia, Kirsty Barclay, David Beers, Alex Blanes, Dominique Browning, Mark Busse, Michael Byers, Fritjof Capra, Ann Cavoukian, Kristin Cavoukian, Sandy Garossino, Mary Gillies, Bill Good, Gerry Hebert, Dr Martha Herbert, Jeff Hopkins, Darren Laur, Susan Linn, Suzanne Little, Margaret McKenzie, Ron McKenzie, Jennie McMordie, Eliza Moat, Janet Newbury, Dr Gwenn O'Keeffe, Maureen Palmer, Charles Pascal, Cecile Petra, Alexandra Samuel, Alyson Schafer, Greg Spendjian, Jim Steyer, Carol Todd, George Tomko, Tracie Wagman, Grant Wilde, Nathan Wilde, and Sandy Wilde.

To Mark Bauerlein, Nicholas Carr, Jaigris Hodson and Sherry Turkle, who read early portions and believed in this book, my special thanks. I'm grateful to Annie Leonard and Ted Smith, who were very helpful with the sustainability portion of the book, which drew substantially on the work of Ted Smith. Thanks also to Kim Wiltzen for her research, Bert Simpson for his steadfast support and advice, and editor Audrey McClellan for her astute guidance. Many thanks for the blessing of my colleagues and friends.

Finally, my thanks to the Lightweb of InfoTech that allowed me to research and write this book. For the speed, convenience and connections made possible via the Net and social media, I'm grateful.

NOTES

INTRODUCTION

1. Joseph Weizenbaum, *Computer Power and Human Reason: From Judgment to Calculation* (San Francisco: W.H. Freeman, 1976).
2. Sherry Turkle, *The Second Self: Computers and the Human Spirit* (Cambridge, MA: MIT Press, 2005), 282.

Part 1 SAFETY

1. The full letter is available on the Red Hood Project website, http://www.redhoodproject.com/the-letter/
2. Raffi Cavoukian and Sandy Garossino, "Cyber Safety by Design: Red Hood Project Demands Action," on the rabble.ca website (among others), December 1, 2012, http://rabble.ca/blogs/bloggers/raffi-cavoukian/2012/11/cyber-safety-design-red-hood-project-demands-action
3. Sandy Garossino, discussion with Parry Aftab and Jian Ghomeshi, on *Q*, CBC Radio, November 19, 2012.
4. Michael Lev-Ram, "Zuckerberg: Kids under 13 Should Be Allowed on Facebook," CNNMoney website, May 20, 2011, http://tech.fortune.cnn.com/2011/05/20/zuckerberg-kids-under-13-should-be-allowed-on-facebook/
5. Anton Troianovski and Shayndi Raice, "Facebook Explores Giving Kids Access," *Wall Street Journal*, June 4, 2012, http://online.wsj.com/article/SB10001424052702303506404577444711741019238.html?mod=WSJ_Tech_LEFTTopNews
6. Ibid.
7. "Statement from Common Sense Media CEO James Steyer on Facebook's Plan to Give Younger Kids Access," June 3, 2012, Common Sense Media website, http://www.commonsensemedia.org/about-us/news/press-releases/statement-from-common-sense-media-ceo-james-steyer-on-facebook%E2%80%99s-plan-t
8. "That Facebook Friend Might Be 10 Years Old, and Other Troubling

News," *Consumer Reports Magazine*, June 2011, http://www.consumer reports. org/cro/magazine-archive/2011/june/electronics-computers /state-of-the-net/facebook-concerns/index.htm

See also Dave McGinn, "Should Children Be Allowed on Facebook?" *Globe and Mail*, September 10, 2012, http://m.theglobeandmail.com /life/the-hot-button/should-children-be-allowed-on-facebook/article 614268/?service=mobile

9. "That Facebook Friend Might Be 10 Years Old."
10. "Internet Safety for Teens, with Personal Protection Systems," ShawTV Central VI, March 6, 2012, http://www.youtube.com/watch?feature =player_embedded&v=QoPe-skp4Nc
11. Ibid.
12. Ibid.
13. Darren Laur, comments at "Cyber Safety: Laws, Parenting, Behaviour," part of the Centre for Child Honouring Speaker Series "Parenting in the Internet Age," Salt Spring Island, BC, November 18, 2012, http://childhonouring.com/uploads/_Dualeventposter-nov8Rev.pdf
14. Bruce Schneier, "The Internet Is a Surveillance State," CNN Opinion website, March 16, 2013, http://www.cnn.com/2013/03/16/opinion /schneier-internet-surveillance/index.html?hpt=hp_c1
15. Dr Cavoukian is also my sister.
16. "Resolution on Privacy by Design," 32nd International Conference of Data Protection and Privacy Commissioners in Jerusalem, October 27–29, 2010, http://www.justice.gov.il/NR/rdonlyres/F8A79347 -170C-4EEF-A0AD- 155554558A5F/26502/ResolutiononPrivacyby Design.pdf
17. Identity, Privacy and Security Initiative website, http://www.ipsi .utoronto.ca/index.html
18. Personal communication with George Tomko, March 2013.
19. Letter posted on the Citizens for Safe Technology website, http:// www.citizensforsafetechnology.org/Martha-Herbert-Letter-WiFi-Bad -Idea-for-Los-Angeles-Schools,45,2901
20. Letter posted on the AAEM website, http://aaemonline.org/images /LettertoLAUSD.pdf
21. Philip J. Landrigan, "Emerging Technologies," in *Pediatric Environmental Health*, 3rd ed. edited by Ruth A. Etzel and Sophie J. Balk (Elk Grove Village, IL: American Academy of Pediatrics, 2011).

22. Philip J. Landrigan, "Our Most Vulnerable," in *Child Honouring: How to Turn This World Around*, edited by Raffi Cavoukian and Sharna Olfman (Salt Spring Island, BC: Homeland Press, 2010), 147, 144.
23. "Cell Phones Are Not Safe for Children," Dr Sanjay Gupta interviewed on *The Dr Oz Show*, January 2013, http://www.youtube.com/watch?v =UG_Jn1RkuYQ
24. "Neurosurgeon: Your Cell Phone Is Not Necessarily a Safe Device," Dr Keith Black interviewed on *PBS News Hour*, PBS, May 31, 2011, http://www.pbs.org/newshour/bb/health/jan-june11/cellphones _05-31.html
25. Declaration of Dr David O. Carpenter, MD, in the civil action of *Morrison vs Portland Public Schools*, US District Court, District of Oregon, Portland Division, June 1, 2011, page 4, http://www.thermoguy.com /pdfs/%5B5%5D%20DECLARATION_OF_DR._DAVID_O._CARPENTER %20_M.D.%20Final%20Draft.pdf

    Dr Carpenter is co-editor (with Cindy Sage) of *The Bioinitiative 2012 Report*, which reviewed over 1,800 new scientific studies into health risks from electromagnetic fields and wireless technologies (radiofrequency radiation). See the press release announcing the report's release at the Bioinitiative 2012 website, http://www.bioinitiative.org /media/press-releases/ and the 1,479-page report itself at http://www.bioinitiative.org/report/wp-content/uploads/pdfs/ BioInitiative Report2012.pdf
26. "Public Health Physician Warns of Smart Meter Dangers...," Dr David Carpenter interviewed by Maine's Smart Meter Safety Coalition, April 29, 2011, http://www.youtube.com/watch?v=n7L21XOC2wA
27. *WiFi in Schools—The Facts,* http://www.youtube.com/watch?v= kmcAXZ-o1K4 (uploaded December 11, 2012, by WiFi in Schools Australia). Learn more about this organization at its website, http://www.wifi-in-schools-australia.org
28. Ibid.
29. Chelsea Clinton and James P. Steyer, "Is the Internet Hurting Children?" CNN Opinion website, May 21, 2012, http://www.cnn.com /2012/05/21/opinion/clinton-steyer-internet-kids

    The full article is in Appendix C of this book.
30. Ibid.
31. Ibid.

32. Ibid.
33. Evgeny Morozov, *The Net Delusion: The Dark Side of Internet Freedom* (New York: PublicAffairs, 2011), 282.

Part 2 INTELLIGENCE

1. David Loye, *Darwin's Lost Theory: Bridge to a Better World* (Pacific Grove, CA: Benjamin Franklin Press, 2007).
2. Abraham Maslow, *Motivation and Personality* (New York: Harper, 1954).
3. The text of this convention is available on the website of the High Commissioner for Human Rights, http://www2.ohchr.org/english/
4. Sherry Turkle, "Connected, But Alone?" TED talk, filmed February 2012, http://www.ted.com/talks/sherry_turkle_alone_together.html
5. Nicholas Carr, *The Shallows: What the Internet Is Doing to Our Brains* (New York: Norton, 2010), 166.
6. Ibid., 116.
7. Mark Bauerlein, ed., *The Digital Divide: Arguments for and against Facebook, Google, Texting, and the Age of Social Networking* (New York: Tarcher/Penguin, 2011).
8. Dimitri Christakis, "Media and Children," TEDxRainier, uploaded December 27, 2011, http://www.youtube.com/watch?v=BoT7qH_uVNo
9. Ibid.
10. Stuart Shanker, keynote speech at BC School Counsellors' Association conference, Connect '12, October 18/19, 2012, uploaded November 7, 2012, http://www.youtube.com/watch?v=N7p2vRt2T1U
11. David Elkind, *The Hurried Child: Growing Up Too Fast Too Soon*, 25th anniversary ed. (Cambridge, MA: Da Capo Press, 2005).
12. Stuart Shanker, keynote speech.
13. Ibid.
14. Carr, *The Shallows*, 116.
15. Neil Postman, *Amusing Ourselves to Death: Public Discourse in the Age of Show Business* (New York: Penguin, 1985), 144.
16. Campaign for a Commercial-Free Childhood, Alliance for Childhood, and Teachers Resisting Unhealthy Children's Entertainment, *Facing the Screen Dilemma: Young Children, Technology and Early Education* (Boston/New York: Campaign for a Commercial-Free Childhood/Alliance

for Childhood, 2012), 3.

17. Personal communication, February 2013. The 25th anniversary edition of *The Plug-In Drug: Television, Computers, and Family Life* was published by Penguin in 2002.
18. Campaign for a Commercial-Free Childhood et al., *Facing the Screen Dilemma*, 5.
19. Ibid.
20. Ibid., 6.
21. Ibid., 8.
22. Ibid., 10.
23. Neil Postman, interview by Charlene Hunter Gault, *MacNeil/ Lehrer NewsHour*, PBS, 1995, http://www.youtube.com/watch ?v=49rcVQ1vFAY
24. Ibid.
25. Mark Prensky, "Digital Natives, Digital Immigrants," *On the Horizon*, MCB University Press, vol. 9, no. 5 (October 2001), http://www.marcprensky. com/writing/prensky%20-%20digital %20natives,%20digital%20immigrants%20-%20part1.pdf
26. Matt Richtel, "A Silicon Valley School That Doesn't Compute," *New York Times*, October 22, 2011, http://www.nytimes.com/2011/10/23 /technology/at-waldorf-school-in-silicon-valley-technology-can-wait .html?_r=0
27. Don Tapscott, *Grown Up Digital: How the Net Generation Is Changing Your World* (New York: McGraw-Hill, 2009), 2. This introductory chapter is available online at http://www.grownupdigital.com/downloads /chapter.pdf

    Also see Tapscott, *Growing Up Digital: The Rise of the Net Generation* (New York: McGraw-Hill, 1998).
28. Tapscott, *Grown Up Digital*, 2, 5, 6.
29. Ibid., 6–7.
30. Fritjof Capra, "Where Have All the Flowers Gone? Reflections on the Spirit and Legacy of the Sixties," December 1, 2002, on Capra's website, http://www.fritjofcapra.net/articles120102.html
31. Ibid.
32. Mark Bauerlein, *The Dumbest Generation: How the Digital Age Stupefies Young Americans and Jeopardizes Our Future* (New York: Tarcher/Penguin, 2008), 234, 235.

33. Personal communication, February 2013.
34. Carr, *The Shallows*, 227.
35. James Steyer, *Talking Back to Facebook: The Common Sense Guide to Raising Kids in the Digital Age* (New York: Scribner, 2012), 6.
36. Ibid., 4, 10.
37. Common Sense Media, "Why We All Need to Talk Back to Facebook," uploaded April 2012, http://vimeo.com/40542873
38. Andrew Keen, *Digital Vertigo: How Today's Online Social Revolution Is Dividing, Diminishing, and Disorienting Us* (New York: St. Martin's Press, 2012).
39. "What Is Second Life," on the Second Life website, http://secondlife.com/whatis/?lang=en-US (accessed January 26, 2013).
40. As he did on national television when performing in the half-time show at the 2012 CFL Grey Cup.
41. "Sext Up Kids—How Children Are Becoming Hyper-Sexualized," *The Current*, CBC Radio, February 23, 2012, http://www.cbc.ca/thecurrent/ episode/2012/02/23/sext-up-kids---how-children-are-becoming-hyper-sexualized/
42. "Sext Up Kids: About This Episode," *Doc Zone*, CBC, http://www.cbc.ca/doczone/episode/sext-up-kids.html
43. Ibid.
44. *Consuming Kids*, Media Education Foundation website, http://www.mediaed.org/cgi-bin/commerce.cgi?preadd=action&key=134
45. Susan Linn, "Honouring Children in Dishonourable Times," in *Child Honouring: How to Turn This World Around*, edited by Raffi Cavoukian and Sharna Olfman (Salt Spring Island, BC: Homeland Press, 2010), 201.
46. Media Education Foundation, *Consuming Kids: The Commercialization of Childhood*, transcript for the documentary (Northampton, MA: MEF, 2008), 3, 20–21, 23, http://www.mediaed.org/assets/products/134/transcript_134.pdf
47. Personal communication, March 2013.
48. Bobbie Johnson, "Privacy No Longer a Social Norm, Says Facebook Founder," *The Guardian*, January 11, 2010, http://www.guardian.co.uk/technology/2010/jan/11/facebook-privacy
49. For a sobering look at this process, see Jeff Saginor, "Meet the Stalkers," *The American Prospect*, April 25, 2013, http://prospect.org/article/meet-stalkers

50. Scott Michelman, "A Good Deal for Facebook, a Bad Deal for Privacy and Kids," Public Citizen Consumer Law and Policy Blog, May 2, 2013, http://pubcit.typepad.com/clpblog/2013/05/a-good-deal-for-facebook - a-bad-deal-for-privacy-and-for-kids.html

    A class action suit against this practice was filed in 2011 and a settlement was reached in 2012, but Public Citizen says the terms of the proposed settlement "are great for Facebook and pretty weak for the 70-million-plus estimated members of the [suit]." Public Citizen has filed objections to the settlement on behalf of six parents and their children, ages 13 to 16, from around the United States, whose photos were used in "sponsored stories."
51. Author's notes of Jaron Lanier's presentation at Social Venture Network conference, spring 1995.
52. Jaron Lanier, "The Reality Club," Edge.org, 2008, http://www.edge.org /3rd_culture/carr08/carr08_index.html#lanier
53. Jaron Lanier, *You Are Not a Gadget: A Manifesto* (New York: Knopf, 2010). And see George Dvorsky, "Why Does Jaron Lanier Hate the Web So Much?" io9.com, December 27, 2012, http://io9.com/5971533 /why-does-jaron-lanier-hate-the-web-so-much
54. Lanier, "The Reality Club."
55. Bill McKibben, *Enough: Staying Human in an Engineered Age* (New York: Henry Holt, 2003), xii, xiii.
56. Ray Kurzweil, "How to Create a Mind," Authors at Google talk, November 16, 2012, http://www.youtube.com/watch?v=zihTWh5i2C4
57. Ray Kurzweil, *The Age of Spiritual Machines: When Computers Exceed Human Intelligence* (New York: Penguin, 1999), http://www.kurzwei lai.net/the-age-of-spiritual-machines-timeline
58. Colin McGinn, "Homunculism," review of *How to Create a Mind: The Secret of Human Thought Revealed*, by Ray Kurzweil (Viking, 2012), *New York Review of Books*, March 21, 2013, http://www.nybooks.com /articles/archives/2013/mar/21/homunculism/?pagination=false
59. *A Day Made of Glass*, CorningIncorporated, uploaded February 7, 2011, http://www.youtube.com/watch?v=6Cf7IL_ eZ38&list=PL36 3989F7 CF53A36
60. *A Day Made of Glass 2: Unpacked. The Story behind Corning's Vision*, CorningIncorporated, uploaded February 3, 2012, http://www.youtube.com/watch?v=X-GXO_urMow

61. Mary Meeker and Liang Wu, KPCB, "2012 Internet Trends," presented at the D10 (All Things Digital) conference, Rancho Palos Verdes, CA, May 30, 2102, http://kpcb.com/insights/2012-internet-trends
62. Evgeny Morozov, *The Net Delusion: The Dark Side of Internet Freedom* (New York: PublicAffairs, 2011).
63. Douglas Rushkoff, *Life Inc.: How Corporatism Conquered the World, and How We Can Take It Back* (New York: Random House, 2011).
64. Postman, *Amusing Ourselves to Death*, vii.
65. Ibid.
66. Humberto Maturana and Pille Bunnell, "The Biology of Business: Love Expands Intelligence," *Reflections* "(Journal of the Society for Organizational Learning) 1, no. 2 (1999).
67. Joseph Chilton Pearce, *Magical Child* (Toronto: Penguin, 1992), 84.
68. Respectful love is the first of nine guiding principles in A Covenant for Honouring Children, http://www.childhonouring.org/covenant principles.html
69. Emotional intelligence is another of the Child Honouring principles.
70. Dan Goleman, *Emotional Intelligence: Why It Can Matter More Than IQ* (New York: Bantam, 1995).
71. See Howard Gardner, *Frames of Mind: The Theory of Multiple Intelligences* (New York: Basic Books, 1983) and *Multiple Intelligences: The Theory in Practice* (New York: Basic Books, 1993).

Part 3 SUSTAINABILITY

The epigraph is a lyric from *Resisto Dancing* (Troubadour Music, 2006), Raffi's CD of motivational songs.

1. You can see the covenant at http://www.childhonouring.org /covenantprinciples.html
2. Kiera Butler, "Your Smartphone's Dirty, Radioactive Secret," *Mother Jones*, November/December 2012, http://www.motherjones.com /environment/2012/11/rare-earth-elements-iphone-malaysia
3. "Rare Earth Elements Markets Worldwide," SBI Energy, June 1, 2011, http://www.sbireports.com/Rare-Earth-Elements-6066525/
4. "Exclusive: Nightline Goes Inside Apple Factories," promo for *Nightline*, ABC, February 19, 2012, http://abcnews.go.com/Nightline/video /exclusive-nightline-inside-apple-factories-china-15749180

5. "Nightline Special Edition—iFactory: Inside Apple," *Nightline*, ABC, February 21, 2012, http://www.youtube.com/watch?v=zqL2nS6GljY
6. Students and Scholars Against Corporate Misbehavior (SACOM), "Apple Fails in Its Responsibility to Monitor Suppliers," February 26, 2013, http://www.scribd.com/doc/127329355/2013-02-26-Apple-Fails-in-Its-Responsibility

   SACOM notes: "Our investigations demonstrate that Apple supplier factories are intensifying a military-style management of workers."
7. You can see the video on the Story of Stuff Project website at http://www.storyofstuff.org/movies-all/story-of-stuff/
8. "FAQ: The Story of Electronics," The Story of Stuff Project website, http://www.storyofstuff.org/movies-all/story-of-electronics/
9. For more on Ray Anderson, see the website of the Ray Anderson Foundation, http://www.raycandersonfoundation.org/
10. Ted Smith, David A. Sonnenfeld, and David N. Pellow, "The Quest for Sustainability and Justice in a High-Tech World," in *Challenging the Chip: Labor Rights and Environmental Justice in the Global Electronics Industry*, edited by Ted Smith, David A. Sonnenfeld, and David N. Pellow (Philadelphia: Temple University Press, 2006), 1.
11. Ibid.
12. Ibid., 3.
13. Ted Smith, author interview on the Temple University Press website, http://www.temple.edu/tempress/authors/1788_qa.html
14. Ibid.
15. Ibid.
16. Ibid.
17. Paul Hawken, *The Ecology of Commerce: A Declaration of Sustainability* (New York: HarperCollins, 1993).
18. Ray Anderson, *Business Lessons from a Radical Industrialist* (New York: St. Martin's Press, 2009), 277.
19. Ibid., 283.
20. Janine Benyus, "The Promise of Biomimicry," TED talk, filmed February 2005, http://www.ted.com/talks/janine_benyus_shares_nature_s_designs.html
21. Ibid.
22. Janine Benyus, "Biomimicry in Action," TEDGlobal talk, filmed July 2009, http://blog.ted.com/2009/08/06/biomimicry_in_a/
23. Al Gore, *Earth in the Balance: Ecology and the Human Spirit* (Boston:

Houghton Mifflin, 1992). In this book, Gore called for ecology to be the central organizing principle in society.

24. Raffi, *The Life of a Children's Troubadour* (Vancouver: Homeland Press, 1999), 300.
25. "What Is Fair Trade?" on the FairTrade Canada website, http://fairtrade.ca/en/about-fairtrade/what-fair-trade
26. Léo Charbonneau, "Secrets to a Satisfying Life," *UA/AU (University Affairs/Affaires universitaires)*, August 8, 2006, http://www.affairesuniversitaires.ca/secrets-to-a-satisfying-life.aspx
27. In conversation with author, April 5, 2013.
28. Annie Leonard, *The Story of Stuff: How Our Obsession with Stuff Is Trashing the Planet, Our Communities, and Our Health—and a Vision for Change* (New York: Free Press, 2010), 63.
29. Adapted from a PowerPoint presentation, "Upstream Opportunities for Electronics," given by Mark Rossi, research director, Clean Production Action, at the International Workshop on Hazardous Substances within the Life Cycle of Electronic and Electrical Products, Vienna, March 29–31, 2011, http://www.cleanproduction.org/library/Mark_Rossi_Vienna_Workshop_ 24mar2011.pdf
30. "Conflict Minerals," Earthworks website, http://www.earthworksaction.org/issues/detail/conflict_minerals#.UXG7tL9GTGt
31. "Conflict Minerals," Enough Project website, http://www.enoughproject.org/conflicts/eastern_congo/conflict-minerals
32. "Conflict Minerals and the Dodd-Frank Act," Earthworks website, http://www.earthworksaction.org/issues/detail/conflict_minerals_and_the_dodd_frank_act
33. For more on ETBC, visit the website at http://www.electronicstakeback.com/home/
34. See also Southwest Network for Environmental and Economic Justice and the Campaign for Responsible Technology, *Sacred Waters: Life-Blood of Mother Earth* (Albuquerque: Southwest Network of EEJ, 1997). Available from Amazon.
35. Dimitri Christakis, "Media and Children," TEDxRainier, uploaded December 27, 2011, http://www.youtube.com/watch?v=BoT7qH_uVNo

CONCLUSION

1. Evgeny Morozov, *The Net Delusion: The Dark Side of Internet Freedom* (New York: PublicAffairs, 2011), 291, 323. For more on the Global Network Initiative, visit the organization's website at http://www.globalnetworkinitiative.org/
2. *The Great Dictator*, directed by Charlie Chaplin (Beverly Hills, CA: United Artists, 1941).
3. Rachel Carson, *Silent Spring* (Boston: Houghton Mifflin, 1962).
4. Marie Winn's books are *The Plug-In Drug: Television, Children, and the Family* (New York: Viking Penguin, 1977), and *Children Without Childhood: Growing Up Too Fast in the World of Sex and Drugs* (New York: Pantheon Books, 1983). An updated version, *The Plug-In Drug: Television, Computers, and Family Life*, was published in 2002 by Penguin.
5. Neil Postman, *Amusing Ourselves to Death: Public Discourse in the Age of Show Business* (New York: Penguin, 1985).
6. This was the title of a radio series prepared by Suzuki for the CBC. In 1991, a book based on the series, titled *It's a Matter of Survival* and written by Anita Gordon and David Suzuki, was published by Harvard University Press.
7. Bill McKibben's books are *Enough: Staying Human in an Engineered Age* (New York: Henry Holt, 2003), and *The End of Nature* (New York: Random House, 1989).
8. Al Gore, *Earth in the Balance: Ecology and the Human Spirit* (Boston: Houghton Mifflin, 1992).
9. The text of the warning is available on the Union of Concerned Scientists website, http://www.ucsusa.org/about/1992-world-scientists.html
10. Quoted in the Vancouver *Province*, May 10, 1992.
11. Raffi Cavoukian, "The Right to a Future," blog post on the Centre for Child Honouring website, January 25, 2011, http://www.childhonouring.org/blog.html?item=109
12. "Justice for Rehtaeh: Demand an Independent Inquiry into the Police Investigation," a petition by Sherri B. on the change.org website, http://www.change.org/en-CA/petitions/justice-for-rehtaeh-demand-an-independent-inquiry-into-the-police-investigation
13. "Stephen Harper to Meet Premier over Rehtaeh Parsons Case," CBC News, April 21, 2013, http://www.cbc.ca/news/canada/nova-scotia

/story/2013/04/21/ns-rehtaeh-parsons-dexter-harper.html

14. Alyson Shontell, "It's Official: Teens Are Bored with Facebook," Business Insider website, March 3, 2013, http://www.businessinsider.com/its-official-teens-are-bored-of-facebook-2013-3
15. Soraya Chemaly, "Facebook's Big Misogyny Problem," *The Guardian*, April 18, 2013, http://www.guardian.co.uk/commentisfree/2013/apr/18/facebook-big-misogyny-problem
16. Victoria Ward, "Toddlers Becoming So Addicted to iPads They Require Therapy," *London Telegraph*, April 21, 2013, http://www.telegraph.co.uk/technology/10008707/Toddlers-becoming-so-addicted-to-iPads-they-require-therapy.html
17. "China Develops Facebook for Children," *Tokyo Times*, April 2013, http://www.tokyotimes.com/2013/china-develops-facebook-for-children/
18. These are some of the same ideas encompassed by A Covenant for Honouring Children. You can see the covenant at http://www.childhonouring.org/covenantprinciples.html
19. Aldous Huxley, *The Perennial Philosophy* (London: Chatto and Windus, 1946; New York: Harper Perennial, 2009).
20. Joel Bakan, *Childhood under Siege: How Big Business Targets Children* (Toronto: Allen Lane Canada, 2011), 16.

APPENDIX B

1. Gary Kovacs, "Tracking the Trackers?" TED talk, filmed February 2012, http://www.ted.com/talks/gary_kovacs_tracking_the_trackers.html

APPENDIX D

1. James Steyer, *Talking Back to Facebook: The Common Sense Guide to Raising Kids in the Digital Age* (New York: Scribner, 2012).
2. His full testimony is available online: Marc Rotenberg, "An Examination of Children's Privacy: New Technologies and the Children's Online Privacy Protection Act (COPPA)" (Washington, DC: Senate Committee on Commerce, Science, and Transportation—Subcommittee on Consumer Protection, Product Safety, and Insurance, 2010), 8, http://epic.org/privacy/kids/EPIC_COPPA_Testimony_042910.pdf

3. Personal communication, March 2013.
4. Canadian Paediatric Society, "Impact of Media Use on Children and Youth," *Paediatric Child Health* 8 no. 5 (May/June 2003): 303, http://www.ncbi.nlm.nih.gov/pmc/articles/PMC2792691/
5. Gwenn Schurgin O'Keeffe, Kathleen Clarke-Pearson and Council on Communications and Media, "The Impact of Social Media on Children, Adolescents, and Families," *Pediatrics* 127, no. 4 (April 1, 2011): 800–804. The full document, with references that have not been included here, is available online at http://pediatrics.aappublications.org/content/127/4/800.full.html

BIBLIOGRAPHY

Anderson, Ray. *Business Lessons from a Radical Industrialist.* New York: St. Martin's Press, 2009.

Anielski, Mark. *The Economics of Happiness: Building Genuine Wealth.* Gabriola Island, BC: New Society Publishers, 2007.

Armstrong, Alison, and Charles Casement. *The Child and the Machine: How Computers Put Our Children's Education at Risk.* Toronto: Key Porter, 1998.

Axness, Marcy. *Parenting for Peace: Raising the Next Generation of Peacemakers.* Boulder, CO: Sentient Publications, 2012.

Bakan, Joel. *Childhood under Siege: How Big Business Targets Children.* Toronto: Allen Lane, 2011.

Bauerlein, Mark. *The Dumbest Generation: How the Digital Age Stupefies Young Americans and Jeopardizes Our Future (Or, Don't Trust Anyone Under 30).* New York: Tarcher/Penguin, 2008.

——— ed. *The Digital Divide: Arguments for and against Facebook, Google, Texting, and the Age of Social Networking.* New York: Tarcher/Penguin, 2011.

Bly, Robert. *The Sibling Society.* New York: Vintage, 1997.

Brazelton, T. Berry, and Stanley I. Greenspan. *The Irreducible Needs of Children: What Every Child Must Have to Grow, Learn, and Flourish.* Cambridge, MA: Perseus, 2000.

Campaign for a Commercial-Free Childhood, Alliance for Childhood, and Teachers Resisting Unhealthy Children's Entertainment. *Facing the Screen Dilemma: Young Children, Technology and Early Education.* Boston/ New York: Campaign for a Commercial-Free Childhood/Alliance for Childhood, 2012.

Carr, Nicholas. *The Shallows: What the Internet Is Doing to Our Brains.* New York: Norton, 2010.

Carson, Rachel. *Silent Spring.* Boston: Houghton Mifflin, 1962.

Cavoukian, Raffi, and Sharna Olfman, eds. *Child Honouring: How to Turn This World Around.* Salt Spring Island, BC: Homeland Press, 2010.

DeGaetano, Gloria. *Parenting Well in a Media Age: Keeping Our Kids Human.*

Fawnskin, CA: Personhood Press, 2004.

Eisler, Riane. *The Real Wealth of Nations: Creating a Caring Economics.* San Francisco: Berrett-Koehler Publishers, 2007.

Elkind, David. *The Hurried Child: Growing Up Too Fast Too Soon.* 25th anniversary edition. Cambridge, MA: Da Capo Press, 2005.

———. *Reinventing Childhood: Raising and Educating Children in a Changing World.* Rosemont, NJ: Modern Learning Press, 1998.

Gardner, Howard. *Frames of Mind: The Theory of Multiple Intelligences.* New York: Basic Books, 1983.

———. *Multiple Intelligences: The Theory in Practice.* New York: Basic Books, 1993.

Gardner, Howard, and Katie Davis. *The App Generation: How Young People Navigate Identity, Intimacy, and Imagination in the Digital Age.* New Haven, CT: Yale University Press, 2013.

Goleman, Dan. *Emotional Intelligence: Why It Can Matter More Than IQ.* New York: Bantam, 1995.

Gopnik, Alison, Andrew N. Meltzoff, and Patricia K. Kuhl. *The Scientist in the Crib: Minds, Brains, and How Children Learn.* New York: Harper Perennial, 2001.

Gordon, Anita, and David Suzuki. *It's a Matter of Survival.* Cambridge, MA: Harvard University Press, 1991.

Gore, Al. *Earth in the Balance: Ecology and the Human Spirit.* Boston: Houghton Mifflin, 1992.

Hansen, James. *Storms of My Grandchildren: The Truth About the Coming Climate Catastrophe and Our Last Chance to Save Humanity.* New York: Bloomsbury USA, 2010.

Hawken, Paul. *The Ecology of Commerce: A Declaration of Sustainability.* New York: HarperCollins, 1993.

Healy, Jane M. *Your Child's Growing Mind: Brain Development and Learning from Birth to Adolescence.* New York: Broadway Books, 2004.

Huxley, Aldous. *The Perennial Philosophy.* New York: Harper Perennial, 2009. First published 1946 by Chatto and Windus.

Keen, Andrew. *Digital Vertigo: How Today's Online Social Revolution Is Dividing, Diminishing, and Disorienting Us.* New York: St Martin's Press, 2012.

Korten, David C. *Agenda for a New Economy: From Phantom Wealth to Real Wealth.* San Francisco: Berrett-Koehler Publishers, 2011.

Kurzweil, Ray. *The Age of Spiritual Machines: When Computers Exceed Human*

Intelligence. New York: Penguin, 1999.
———. *How to Create a Mind: The Secret of Human Thought Revealed.* New York: Viking, 2012.
Lakoff, George. *The Political Mind: A Cognitive Scientist's Guide to Your Brain and Its Politics.* New York: Penguin, 2009.
Lanier, Jaron. *You Are Not a Gadget: A Manifesto.* New York: Knopf, 2010.
Ledoux, Joseph. *The Emotional Brain: The Mysterious Underpinnings of Emotional Life.* New York: Touchstone, 1998.
———. *Synaptic Self: How Our Brains Become Who We Are.* New York: Viking Penguin, 2002.
Leonard, Annie. *The Story of Stuff: How Our Obsession with Stuff Is Trashing the Planet, Our Communities, and Our Health—And a Vision for Change.* New York: Free Press, 2010.
Levin, Diane E., and Jean Kilbourne. *So Sexy So Soon: The New Sexualized Childhood and What Parents Can Do to Protect Their Kids.* New York: Ballantine Books, 2008.
Levine, Mel. *A Mind at a Time: America's Top Learning Expert Shows How Every Child Can Succeed.* New York: Simon & Schuster, 2012.
Linn, Susan. *Consuming Kids: The Hostile Takeover of Childhood.* New York: The New Press, 2004.
Loye, David. *Darwin's Lost Theory: Bridge to a Better World.* Pacific Grove, CA: Benjamin Franklin Press, 2007.
Maslow, Abraham. *Motivation and Personality.* New York: Harper, 1954.
McKibben, Bill. *The End of Nature.* New York: Random House, 1989.
———. *Enough: Staying Human in an Engineered Age.* New York: Henry Holt, 2003.
McLuhan, Marshall. *Understanding Media: The Extensions of Man.* Cambridge, MA: MIT Press, 1994.
Morozov, Evgeny. *The Net Delusion: The Dark Side of Internet Freedom.* New York: PublicAffairs, 2011.
Pearce, Joseph Chilton. *Magical Child.* Toronto: Penguin, 1992.
Postman, Neil. *Amusing Ourselves to Death: Public Discourse in the Age of Show Business.* New York: Penguin, 1985.
———. *The Disappearance of Childhood.* New York: Vintage, 1994.
Putnam, Robert. *Bowling Alone: The Collapse and Revival of American Community.* New York: Touchstone, 2001.

Rushkoff, Douglas. *Life Inc.: How Corporatism Conquered the World, and How We Can Take It Back*. New York: Random House, 2011.

———. *Present Shock: When Everything Happens Now.* New York: Penguin, 2013.

Schmidt, Eric, and Jared Cohen. *The New Digital Age: Reshaping the Future of People, Nations and Business.* New York: Knopf, 2013.

Siegel, Daniel J. *The Developing Mind: How Relationships and the Brain Interact to Shape Who We Are.* New York: Guilford Press, 1999.

Smith, Ted, David A. Sonnenfeld, and David N. Pellow, eds. *Challenging the Chip: Labor Rights and Environmental Justice in the Global Electronics Industry*. Philadelphia: Temple University Press, 2006.

Steyer, James. *The Other Parent: The Inside Story of the Media's Effect on Our Children.* New York: Atria Books, 2002.

———. *Talking Back To Facebook: The Common Sense Guide to Raising Kids in the Digital Age.* New York: Scribner, 2012.

Turkle, Sherry. *Alone Together: Why We Expect More from Technology and Less from Each Other*. New York: Basic Books, 2011.

———. *The Second Self: Computers and the Human Spirit.* Cambridge, MA: MIT Press, 2005.

Weaver, Andrew. *Keeping Our Cool: Canada in a Warming World.* Toronto: Penguin Canada, 2008.

Weizenbaum, Joseph. *Computer Power and Human Reason: From Judgment to Calculation.* San Francisco: W.H. Freeman, 1976.

Winn, Marie. *Children Without Childhood: Growing Up Too Fast in the World of Sex and Drugs.* New York: Pantheon, 1983.

———. *The Plug-In Drug: Television, Computers, and Family Life.* 25th anniversary edition. New York: Penguin, 2002.

Wolf, Maryanne. *Proust and the Squid: The Story and Science of the Reading Brain*. New York: Harper Perennial, 2008.

Young-Bruehl, Elisabeth. *Childism: Confronting Prejudice Against Children.* New Haven, CT: Yale University Press, 2012.

INDEX

INDEX

Raffi Cavoukian, C.M., O.B.C.

A renowned singer known by his first name alone, Raffi was a pioneer in quality recordings for kids on his indie label, Troubadour. For millions of fans, Raffi's music was the soundtrack of their childhoods, and they took his signature song, "Baby Beluga," to heart. These "beluga grads" now share his music with their own kids. Raffi has been described by the *Washington Post* and the *Toronto Star* as the most popular children's entertainer in the Western world, and Canada's all-time children's champion. Raffi is a music producer, author, entrepreneur, and ecology advocate. He is the recipient of numerous honours, including the Global 500 Roll and the Order of Canada. He holds three honorary degrees and is a member of the Club of Budapest.

In a career spanning four decades, Raffi has refused all commercial endorsement offers and has never taken part in direct advertising to children. He is a passionate supporter of a commercial-free childhood. In 2006, he was awarded the Fred Rogers Integrity Award.

In 2010, Raffi founded the Centre for Child Honouring on Salt Spring Island, BC (childhonouring.org), a global movement that views honouring children as the best way to create sustainable, peacemaking cultures.

In 2012, Raffi and the Centre co-founded Red Hood Project, a movement for online security for children and youth (redhoodproject.com).

#lightwebdarkweb

The initial impetus for this book came from Raffi's response to the suicide of Vancouver teen Amanda Todd after years of online harassment. The book is dedicated to Amanda. amandatoddlegacy.org